paul gayler

a passion for cheese

paul gayler

a passion for cheese

more than 130 innovative ways to cook with cheese

with a foreword by juliet harbutt

with photographs by gus filgate

kyle cathie limited

This revised edition published 2007 by
Kyle Cathie Limited
122 Arlington Road
London
NW1 7HP
www.kylecathie.com

First published in 1997 by Kyle Cathie Limited

ISBN 978 1 85626 705 2

Copyright © Paul Gayler 1997
Colour photographs copyright © Gus Filgate 1997
Black & white photographs copyright © Nic Barlow 1997

Paul Gayler is hereby identified as the author of this work in
accordance with Section 77 of the Copyright, Designs and
Patents Act, 1988

A Cataloguing in Publication record for this title is available
from the British Library

Home economy by Louise Pickford, assisted by Zoë Sharp
Styling by Penny Markham
Book design by Geoff Hayes

The publishers wish to thank Michael Day of the Huge
Cheese Company for his donation of the cheeses used in
the photographs, and the Guilde des Fromagers for
permission to reproduce their logo.

contents

foreword

Cheese is a combination of man's ingenuity and one of Mother Nature's finest miracles, milk, and it never ceases to amaze me that from something so simple and so natural thousands of cheeses are made around the world. Each with their own unique flavour, character and texture is a reflection of the soil, the grazing, the breed of animal and the passion and skill of the cheesemaker and should be enjoyed first and foremost on its own with maybe a glass of wine and some wonderful local bread.

However, cheese is also one of the most versatile ingredients available to a chef or cook and can turn the simplest or mundane dish into a gastronomic sensation. Imagine pasta without Parmigiano-Reggiano or French cuisine without their soft, aromatic goat's cheeses or spicy Roquefort? Some dishes, like cheese on toast, cheese omelette or souffle, can be made with almost any cheese. Others like Fondue or Greek salad rely on the unique texture and taste of specific cheeses so if the chef does not have an in-depth knowledge and understanding of the different cheeses the end result will fall well short of perfection when a substitute is used.

In the last 15 years I have seen endless cookery books and TV programmes featuring recipes with cheese but most are simply old recipes revamped to sell another book. The choice of cheeses is seemingly arbitrary, often ill chosen and simply demonstrates how little the writer cares or understands about how cheese interacts or marries with other ingredients. Too often generic names like 'chevre' or blue cheeses are used, which in most cases is as pointless as saying fruit instead of apple, or lettuce instead of cos [Romaine] lettuce in a Caesar salad.

Paul Gayler however, is genuinely passionate about cheese and has taken time to create dishes that will bring out the best in the cheese or chosen cheeses that truly enhance the dish. Best of all he actually names the cheeses and offers alternatives, rather than using generic names, and has given a modern twist to some traditional dishes like Saltimbocca.

Paul brings to the book the same professionalism and enthusiasm that has won him the respect of his contemporaries in the highly competitive restaurant world and those who work with him in his kitchen at The Lanesborough in London. The layout and Paul's style of writing is straightforward, practical and easy to follow but is also imaginative, inspirational and beautifully photographed making it the perfect gift for anyone who loves cheese.

Juliet Harbutt
www.thecheeseweb.com

introduction

When I wrote A Passion for Cheese, I wanted to celebrate the remarkable variety of superb cheeses that had recently become available, and in particular the renaissance in farmhouse cheesemaking. I could never have imagined that, a decade later, the revolution would have continued apace, with even more cheeses appearing on the market and a whole new generation of specialist shops opening up.

Perhaps the biggest change in the way we eat now is that we are more interested in where our food comes from. Good restaurants make a point of sourcing local food and are proud to state its provenance on their menus. Many consumers like to shop at farmers' markets or go direct to the farm to buy produce, which provides the opportunity to talk to the people who actually produce the food and also to escape from industrialised, mass-produced ingredients and enjoy something with a little individuality.

Farmhouse cheese is one of the big success stories of local, artisan food. In fact it has recently been claimed that there are now more cheeses made in the UK than in France! Small-scale cheesemakers tend to use milk from their own herd and make the cheese on-farm in their own dairies. It's the ideal product to sell locally – indeed, some soft cheeses have such a short shelf life that they have to be sold locally. Quality is all-important and the quality of cheese depends on the breed of animal, be it cow, sheep or goat, the pasture on which it has grazed and the skill of the cheesemaker. Because of this, we know when we buy farmhouse cheese that we are buying something truly special.

With the growth of artisan cheeses, more specialist cheese shops are opening up, and you can even shop on the internet, purchasing all your cheese by mail order. Supermarkets remain the least interesting place to buy cheese, ignoring small-scale cheesemakers, who can't produce the kind of quantities they require. I would like to see more done in future to give small producers the opportunity to sell their produce in local supermarkets. Perhaps, because of the increasing number of cheeses available, we are now more willing to experiment with new varieties. Cow's milk cheese is perennially popular but sales of goat's cheese are on the increase. Mediterranean cheeses have become more popular than ever too, with classics such as Parmesan and brie becoming staples to rival Cheddar and Stilton.

With such a wealth of wonderful cheeses accessible, the creative possibilities for cooking are endless. It seems to me that cheese's unique characteristics in cooking are too often overlooked. Why not pair blue cheese with white fish, or Cheddar with a lobster bisque? Use goat's cheese to make a pesto sauce? Add Sage Derby to a stuffing for quail? These are just some of the unlikely-sounding combinations in this book that have turned out to be real winners. But let's not forget old favourites either, such as Gruyère scattered over a vegetable gratin, the salty bite of feta in a Greek salad, and cool, creamy buffalo's milk mozzarella with tomatoes and basil.

My passion for cheese has lasted throughout my career, and every time I discover a new variety I find it impossible to resist the urge to take it into the kitchen and experiment. I very much hope that reading this book will inspire you to do likewise.

how cheese is made

Cheese could be described as an inspired collaboration between Man and Nature. Part of my fascination with it stems from the astonishing diversity that is created out of a single product – milk. Consider the sheer scope and variety of the world's cheese. Then consider that they all are made from milk – many from cow's milk but some from the milk of goats, sheep, water buffalo and even, in some remote areas, donkeys and horses.

The magical property of milk that enables us to turn it into cheese is its ability to curdle. This is said to have been discovered accidentally by Arab nomads many centuries ago, when a bag of ewe's milk was cut open to reveal a curd-like substance. The heat from the sun had turned the milk sour, causing it to coagulate. Nowadays, most cheese is made from milk that has been pasteurized, that is heated to 72°C (162°F) for just 15 seconds and then cooled rapidly to 31°C (88°F). This destroys the bacteria that cause the milk to sour and curdle, so rennet has to be added to induce coagulation.

Pasteurization is a controversial subject, with many cheese connoisseurs believing that a great cheese can only be made from unpasteurized or 'raw' milk, since this contains the bacteria that contribute to the cheese's flavour and character. On the other hand, food technologists will argue that pasteurized milk is 'clean' milk. This may be the case in factory cheesemaking, where milk is collected in large tankers from a number of different suppliers, making it difficult to monitor the quality of the raw product. But farmhouse cheese is usually made from milk produced on the farm, giving the cheesemaker complete control over its quality.

The uniform character of pasteurized milk enables the cheesemaker to achieve a consistent product, which can reach a very high standard. But the truth is that the majority of great cheeses are made from unpasteurized milk, although there are some surprising exceptions to the rule, such as Colston Bassett Stilton.

Besides the type of milk used, many factors influence the character of each cheese, from the pasture, breed of animal, climate and even the time of year, to the way the curds are cut, the shaping, and the maturing process.

Once the milk has been soured, usually with a starter culture, rennet may be added and the milk clots into a fairly solid junket. This needs to be cut up to allow the whey to drain out. For softer cheeses, the curd is lightly cut and then left to drain naturally. For hard cheeses it is cut finely and then in some cases such as for Parmesan, scalded, or 'cooked', at 41-45°C (105-130°F) so that it becomes dense and more whey can be drained off. The curd settles at the bottom of the vat, where it is milled again into small pieces.

Other than the softest cream and cottage cheeses, all chesses are salted with either dry salt or brine. Some soft and semi-soft varieties are also sprayed and washed with various solutions or with bacteria. Such measures encourage certain styles of ripening and the formation of particular types of rind.

The curd is ladled into suitable moulds and pressed. Hard, compressed cheese is pressed heavily, while the curd may be left to firm naturally or only lightly pressed for most soft and semi-soft ripened cheeses.

Unripened cheese such as cottage cheese or fromage blanc are eaten fresh but most cheeses go through a final stage of ripening, or maturing. This crucial process allows cheese to develop its character with time – from as little as four weeks for a Camembert to as much as four years for a Parmesan. During ripening, which takes place in a controlled atmosphere, the microbes and enzymes change their composition. Each stage contributes to the final character of the cheese and is carefully monitored by the cheesemaker.

choosing and storing cheese

Always try to buy cheese from a specialist merchant, who will give good advice and, usually, allow you to sample what's on offer. Go for farmhouse cheeses, which tend to be far more interesting in character and flavour than plastic-wrapped, factory-produced ones. Whenever practical, purchase whole cheeses or blocks of a decent size. Small portions can lose their flavour quickly.

Advice on storing individual types of cheese is given on the following pages, but there are a few general guidelines to bear in mind:

The ideal storage place is a cool larder or cellar, about 10-15°C (50-60°F). This idyllic atmosphere neither retards the flavour nor hinders any ripening process. Nowadays, however, most people are resigned to storing cheese in the refrigerator. In this case, select the least cold part and aim for a temperature of 7-9°C (45-48°F).

If you do store cheese in the refrigerator, place each one in a separate airtight container. Certain varieties, notably the strong-smelling ones, are best wrapped in foil first. Avoid plastic film as it makes cheese sweat. Any cheese sold in its own box, Camembert for example, should be stored in the box. I never freeze cheese, as all too often this gives it a dry, grainy texture.

hard and semi-hard cheeses

Hard cheeses are ones that have been heavily pressed to give them a dense texture. The hardest include the extra-firm Italian grana cheeses, of which Parmigiano Reggiano, commonly known as Parmesan, is the most highly esteemed. Wonderful for grating, the grana cheeses also include grana pandana and pecorino Romano, which is made from sheep's milk.

At the softer end of the range are the semi-hard cheeses, which include Tilsit, Danbo, Samsow, Manchego, California's Monterey Jack, and Lancashire – of which the finest is probably Kirkham's Lancashire, one of my favourite cheeses.

Somewhere in the middle of the hard and semi-hard category is a huge grouping that includes three sub-groups: Cheddar-type cheese, Gouda-type and Gruyère-type.

Cheddar-type cheeses are cooked, pressed cheeses of middling firmness. They are prized all over the world for their sweet, full flavour and culinary adaptability. Hence it is possible to find Cheddars of English, American, Canadian, Australian and New Zealand origin. France's equivalent is Cantal. However, the only true Cheddars are the great English farmhouse cheese, such as Montgomery's and Keen's from Somerset. Other cheeses related to this family are crumbly, piquant Cheshire (I am particularly fond of Appleby's Cheshire); very crumbly mild Caerphilly, of which the supreme example is Duckett's Caerphilly; mellow Double Gloucester, orange-hued Leicester and mottled-green Sage Derby, whose curds are infused with liquid sage extract.

Gouda-type cheeses are typically straw-coloured with a thin rind and a coating of paraffin wax. Although Holland's authentic Gouda continues to be made in the town of that name near Amsterdam, other countries produce versions of it under an assortment of names – Teifi (Welsh), Broodkaas (Belgian) and German Gouda. Similar to Gouda is Edam, which is made of partially skimmed milk and therefore popular with those who count calories.

Gruyère-type cheeses range in flavour from a mellow nuttiness to a rich, full taste that is almost fruity and sweet. Their characteristic holes are formed by adding the popolonic acid bacterium. Swiss Gruyère has tiny pinprick holes spaced so far apart that they are sometimes difficult to see. Comté, Appenzell and fontina have virtually no holes at all. The Norwegian cheese Jarlsberg has large holes, eclipsed only by the huge ones of Emmenthal.

Gruyère-type cheeses are invaluable in the kitchen. They grate cleanly and effortlessly, melt down rapidly and smoothly, and lend their fine, nutty flavour to a dish without overwhelming the other ingredients.

Choosing and Storing

Even the hardest of grana cheeses should be moist. The rind and surface should not be cracked, neither should the surface show signs of sweating. Avoid Cheddar-types that are darker near the rind or at their cut edges, as this may indicate that they have dried out. Never buy pre-grated grana cheeses: no matter how fresh they claim to be, the flavour will deteriorate within hours.

Grana cheese such as Parmesan that you intend to use for grating will keep very well double-wrapped in foil in the refrigerator. Hard and semi-hard cheeses for the cheeseboard should, ideally, be stored in a cool larder, with the cut surfaces covered by foil and the crust free to breathe. Failing that, store them as for grana cheeses for grating. They will keep well in the refrigerator for at least a week but no more than two. Bring them to room temperature before serving.

soft and semi-soft ripened cheeses

These have a high water content and undergo a similar ripening process to hard cheeses. Soft ripened cheeses contain 50-70 per cent water, are spreadable and include Brie, Camembert, Bonchester and Pencarreg. Semi-soft ripened cheeses, such as Bel Paese, Gubbeen and Reblochon, contain 40-50 per cent water and often feel springy to the touch.

Because they are moist and therefore more susceptible to microbes than hard cheeses, they ripen in a matter of weeks rather than months. Unlike hard cheeses, which are ripened from within by adding a starter bacteria to them, soft ripened cheeses are ripened from the outside, by the action of a surface mould which is sprayed on after salting. In order to create a bloomy white rind, such as the one on Brie, Camembert and Coulommiers, the cheese is sprayed with the mould Penicillium candidum. The relatively mild, creamy characteristics of semi-soft cheese such as Bel Paese and Morbier are achieved by washing the rind with a brine that slows down bacterial development.

Some semi-soft varieties, such as Port Salut, Münster and Reblochon, are known as monastery cheeses because they are ripened by a method developed by Trappist monks. The rind is washed with solutions that include alcohol – usually wine, beer or liqueur – resulting in a tangy flavour, savoury aroma and distinctive rind. Nowadays a culture of Breyibacterium linens might be used instead. This creates a thin, yellowish-red bacterial growth on the rind, which is not eaten.

Choosing and Storing

Soft ripened cheese with white bloomy rinds should never smell of ammonia, nor should their rind show signs of hardness or browning. The paste should not ooze excessively. Ripe, whole cheeses should feel springy to the touch. The paste of cut wedges should look plump and even textured; a chalky line indicates underripeness.

Semi-soft ripened cheeses, including the monastery varieties, should possess a fruity – but never rank – aroma and feel slightly elastic. The rind should look fresh and ungummy.

soft fresh cheeses

pasta filata cheeses

Store soft and semi-soft ripened cheeses wrapped – or in the case of monastery cheeses doubled-wrapped – in foil in an airtight box in the refrigerator. The soft cheese Vacherin Mont d'Or is a case apart: it should never be refrigerated. You should keep it in a cool, damp place and press a block of wood against cut surfaces to prevent them running.

Bring soft ripened varieties to room temperature for two hours before serving. Once fully ripe they stay at their best for only a day or two. Semi-soft ripened cheeses such as Bel Paese keep for up to ten days, while the monastery cheeses vary in their keeping ability – from two to three days for Pont l'Évêque and up to a week for Reblochon.

These are uncooked and unripened cheeses. Uncooked means that the curds are not heated in their whey, which would encourage them to harden and cohere, while unripened indicated that the cheeses have not been ripened for more than a few days. They are too young to have developed any rind. Most soft fresh cheeses are made from cow's milk, often skimmed of its fat. Examples include cottage cheeses, curd cheese, fromage frais, fromage blanc, quark and American pot cheese.

Fresh ricotta, one of the gems of Piedmont, is different. Traditionally it is prepared from the whey left over from sheep's milk after making pecorino. However, sometimes the whey from other cheeses, including cow's milk varieties is used. Ricotta's dry, bland texture makes it ideal for blending with other ingredients in both savoury and sweet dishes.

Cream cheese is, as the name implies, made from cream rather than milk. One of the most celebrated examples is mascarpone, which was originally made only in Lombardy in autumn and winter. It is created from cream that has been skimmed from whole milk. Once its curds have formed, they are drained for about 24 hours and then whipped to a texture like very thick double cream. Mascarpone tastes delicate and slightly sweet and has many culinary uses, its affinity with fruit and chocolate only being surpassed by its empathy with savoury ingredients.

Choosing and Storing

These cheeses should look and smell very fresh, clean and white, with no grubby edges. On no account should they ever taste bitter. Ricotta bought loose from a good Italian delicatessen or cheese shop has an incomparable sweet, fresh flavour that bears no resemblance to the type sold in tubs. It must be eaten within a day or two, as the flavour becomes quickly tainted. All soft fresh cheeses are highly perishable. If possible, use a cool bag to carry them home and then put them on the coldest shelf of the fridge. Very moist types of ricotta, cottage and curd cheese benefit from being stored in the fridge on a draining plate covered with a bowl. The drier fresh cheeses, including cream cheese, can be placed directly in an airtight container – lined with wax paper or foil. Use soft fresh cheese within four days.

Pasta filata is an Italian term meaning 'spun paste' and refers to a technique of immersing the curd in hot water or whey, then kneading and stretching it. Well known Pasta filata cheeses include mozzarella, a semi-soft, unripened cheese made with the milk of cows or water buffalo; provolone, a ripened cheese that is available as a mild dolce or a stronger-tasting piccante; and Caciocavello, which is also ripened, often smoked, and can be just firm enough to slice when young or hard enough to grate when mature. All such cheeses are widely used in the Italian kitchen, especially for toppings, fillings and stuffings.

Choosing and Storing

If bought loose from an Italian grocer, mozzarella should have an immaculately white colour and a fresh, lactic smell. Otherwise, buy the type sold in a little sachet of whey rather than the dry, plastic-wrapped ones. Buffalo's milk mozzarella is considered superior to cow's milk because of its stronger flavour and softer, less rubbery texture. Provolone should possess a faint, lactic aroma. With both provolone and Caciocavello, look for a fine glossy rind and avoid holes in the paste, as these may indicate internal fermentation.

Mozzarella bought loose should immediately be immersed in milk, left in the refrigerator and consumed within five days. With supermarket versions in their sealed bags of whey, honour the use-by date and keep any partially used portions in the whey in a dish. Store provolone and Caciocavello double-wrapped in foil. Provolone will keep well for one week in a cool place or the refrigerator and Caciocavello for up to two weeks.

goat's cheeses

Ranging in texture from soft and creamy to dry and sliceable, goat's milk cheeses are now made in countries all over the world. In France they are known as chèvre, the generic term for such cheeses. While they all share a dry, piquant aftertaste, their tangy- and unmistakably 'goaty' – flavour varies in strength according to the region of production, altitude, ripening period and mould cultures.

Traditionally produced on small farms or co-operatives throughout France and the Mediterranean, chèvre is made into a variety of small shapes: logs (bûches), dainty cylinders (bûchettes), little bells (clochettes) and an assortment of pyramids, discs and so on. The name crottin – which, you may or may not wish to know, means horse droppings! – refers to the shape of the small, hard, round goat's cheeses and also to their slightly darker colouring. Crottin de Chavignol is the best-known example and is highly prized for its bracingly sharp, full flavour.

In recent years goat's cheeses have become very popular in Britain, Australia and the United States, with many small cheesemakers producing their own unique versions. Montrachet is possibly the best-known American variety, while Kervella is produced in Western Australia and Chabis, Golden Cross, Roubiliac, Tymsboro' and many others in Britain.

Choosing and Storing
Because there is such diversity and seasonal variance within this group, it is best to sample before you buy, That way you will be sure that the degree of tartness, ripeness, dryness, and so on is to your taste. Autumn and spring are particularly good times to buy, although crottin de Chavignol tends to be better in winter. Avoid tough-looking rinds unless, of course, you want a well-aged crottin. Don't buy cheese with messy colouring or a rancid smell. Many goat's cheeses are sold slightly underripe. Bear in mind that they will continue to mature and will ripen quickly if left beneath a cloche at a room temperature of, say 20°C (68°F). If you want to hold the cheese at a particular stage of maturity, wrap it in foil and store it in an airtight container in the fridge. Most goat's cheese will keep well in this way for at least a week.

blue cheeses

Blue cheeses acquire their characteristic veining from mould spores. These may be introduced to the milk before it is soured and then encouraged to develop during ripening, when the cheese is pierced with fine needles. This allows the air in so the mould can spread.

The most noble blur cheese must surely be Roquefort. Some 2,000 years ago it acquired its veining from the natural Penicillium glaucum, which thrived in the limestone caves of the Combalou plateau in France. In 1411 Charles VI bestowed a royal charter upon these caves, thereby initiating the Roquefort appellation, or quality control, which still exists today. Unusually for a blue cheese, Roquefort is made with sheep's milk, which is partly responsible for its pungent flavour. In cookery, its assertiveness works wonderfully well with other robust ingredients.

Italy's champion blue cheese is Gorgonzola, which is milder, softer and less salty than Roquefort. Both cheeses have very little rind.

Britain's most illustrious example is Stilton, of which the finest is Colston Basset Stilton. It has a distinctive rind and is moist and creamy. More recent British blues include Dunsyre Blue (cow's milk) and Lanark Blue (sheep's milk) from Scotland, and Beenleigh Blue (sheep's milk) from Devon.

Ireland's most famous is Cashel Blue which, like Roquefort and Gorgonzola, has a foil-wrapped rind. Its particularly creamy texture blends smoothly in cooking. Other soft-textured blues that cook well include the American Oregon Blue and Maytag Blue.

Choosing and Storing
Choose Roquefort in its prime, that is from around six months old. In perfect condition it will have a creamy, moist, virtually white paste and a uniform greenish-blue veining. It should have just a faint smell of mould. These guidelines apply to most blue cheese that are wrapped in foil, except their paste is not quite as ivory-white as that of Roquefort and some of them reach maturity at only three months.

Gorgonzola should be springy to the touch and never brownish and hard. Contrary to popular belief, it should not have a pungent smell. Stilton should be creamy-ivory, with an even distribution of greenish-blue veining. It should be open-textured and never dry, hard or salty.

Wrap all foil-finished blue cheeses except Gorgonzola in a double layer of foil and keep them in an airtight container in the refrigerator. Gorgonzola is better wrapped in a damp cloth and stored in a cool place. All these cheeses should stay in good condition for 8 to 12 days. Be sure to bring them back to room temperature before serving.

The best way to store Stilton is wrapped in a linen cloth in a cool cellar or larder. Moisten the cloth if the cheese starts to dry out. If these conditions are impracticable, store it as for Roquefort.

the cheeseboard

The cheeseboard in a good restaurant will offer 10 to 15 varieties of cheese, chosen for their different characters and strengths. At home, it is better to have a small selection of cheeses in their prime than a large number in poor condition. A small selection is also less confusing to the palate, enabling your guests to relish each cheese to the full. It generally makes sense to offer one hard or semi-hard cheese, one semi-soft and one blue.

If possible, buy from a good cheese shop, where the cheeses are properly stored and staff will be able to advise you. As a change, it can be fun to put together an alternative cheeseboard – see pages 183-9 for ideas.

Bring refrigerated cheese to room temperature for at least an hour before serving to allow the full flavour to develop. However, the prepared cheeseboard should not be left in a warm room for more than 40 minutes, otherwise the cheeses may sweat. One way of overcoming this is to put the cheeses on the board and cover them with a damp cloth. I like only wooden boards, and I provide a separate knife for each cheese to prevent the different flavours intermingling.

There is an art to cutting cheese so that the cheeseboard continues to look appetizing and wastage is minimized. Small square or round cheeses, such as Camembert, should be cut in half (diagonally if it is a square cheese) and then into small triangular wedges. It used to be considered bad manners to cut the 'nose' off a wedge of brie, and it certainly leaves an unappetizing piece of rind. Instead, long slices should be taken from alternate sides so that it maintains its shape. Tall, thin pieces of cheese, such as a wedge from a whole Cheddar, can be laid on their side, making it easier to cut off long slices. Finally, truckles such as Stilton need to have a 'lid' cut off the top. You can then either slice off whole rounds or score a line round the cheese a few centimetres from the top and cut down to give small wedges. Replace the lid when storing the cheese.

What to serve with cheese? I prefer something simple such as crusty bread and perhaps some tart grapes, crisp apples or ripe pears. I avoid biscuits and butter since I am not convinced that they enhance the cheese. Occasionally, though, I do like to serve a good chutney with a farmhouse Cheddar or similar cheese (see pages 186-8).

how to taste cheese

Before tasting, always allow the cheese to come to room temperature. This allows the aromas and flavours to be at their maximum potential.

Milder cheeses should be tasted first, then contintue with some stronger flavoured ones. Leave full flavoured blue-veined and pungent 'stinky' cheese until last.

Ideally, you should taste each cheese at its centre first, working your way to the outside, where the cheese will be the most aged and consequently the strongest in flavour.

I always start tasting from the tip of my tongue, working the cheese towards the back of the mouth. This way the cheese forms individual flavour characteristics as it comes into contact with the flavour sense areas, ie. sweet, salty, sour, hot etc.

When tasting cheese, consider:

Texture – smooth, grainy, supple

Density – how compact it feels in your mouth

Flavour – how flavoursome is the cheese, is it clean, cloying, mild, strong, fruity?

Acidity – is it lemony?

Finish – do the flavour characteristics linger in the mouth (similar to that of wine)?

Saltiness – is the cheese well-balanced?

Conclusion flavours – earthy, nutty, toasted, grassy, mushroomy, creamy, pungent, piquant

Aroma – smell the cheese, get a feel for its aroma, as you would with a wine

serving wine with cheese

Alain Senderens, the well-known Parisian chef-restaurateur, regards the partnership of cheese and wine as so important that he displays a list of famous cheese and wine marriages in his restaurant. Ultimately, however, personal taste should play a part – although a few general rules hold good, such as strong cheeses need a full-bodied wine while mild ones are better matched with a light wine.

One common fallacy that I am happy to ignore is that all cheese goes with all red wine. This isn't the case. You must take into account the individual nature of both the cheese and the wine. Blanket statements about cheese and wine being good companions refer to everyday or indifferent wines. Certainly if a wine has negative qualities, these will be masked by cheese, especially a strong-flavoured one. By the same token, a powerful cheese will overwhelm the exquisite subtleties of a fine wine.

That said, there are many magical partnerships that are very easy to get right, particularly if you are looking for a match for a decent red wine – perhaps one that has been carried over from the main course. In this case, you could choose from the many hard and semi-hard cheeses, such as Gruyère, Beaufort, Comté, Emmenthal, Appenzel, mild Cheddar, Cheshire and fontina to name a few. You might also pick your way carefully around the semi-soft and soft cheeses, Among the soft fermented cheeses, Reblochon and Pont l'Évêque are probably the best bet, but only if they have been well cared for and remain delicate – almost sweet – in flavour. Be very cautious if you want to include Camembert and Brie; when ripe, these cheese can acquire an acrid taste of ammonia that will kill good wine. It is best not to buy them too far in advance because they deteriorate rapidly after a day or two.

If you are serving a Sancerre or Pouilly Fumé with the main course and suspect it will be carried over to the cheese course, then you have the opportunity to enjoy one of the world's most sublime cheese and wine alliances, that of white goat's cheese and flinty white wine. With a selection of at least six goat's milk cheeses, you can create a cheeseboard that is visually very exciting, particularly if you line the board, or a large flat-bottomed basket, with glossy green vine leaves, or plane tree or chestnut leaves.

One of the great challenges of the cheeseboard is finding a match for strong, salty, blue cheese, whose aggressive nature has a distinctly discouraging effect on fine red wines. Roquefort, for example, despite its wondrous qualities, will completely annihilate most wines. However, most blue cheeses – and Roquefort in particular – make good partners for Sauternes and other dessert wines. So you can serve Sauternes with the dessert course, then continue the wine into the cheese course.

If you don't plan to offer a desert wine, port goes well with strong blues, especially Stilton. If you're particularly keen on having a red wine, you could try a powerful, full-bodied one such as Zinfandel or, for special occasions, Gigondas or Côte Rotie.

A young-to-middle-aged Gorgonzola or Bresse Bleu, or a milder blue such as dolcelatte or dolcelatte torta, is a good match for a Zinfandel, Barolo or Barbaresco. A well-aged Gorgonzola, however, would probably be too challenging in its pungency and sharpness even for such robust wines.

cooking with cheese

All cheeses have unique characteristics but there are a few points to bear in mind when deciding which to cook with. Generally I find I use fresh cheeses more in summer for light dishes and desserts and in winter harder cheeses, which add warmth and depth of flavour. Hard cheeses such as Parmesan, Cheddar and Gruyère are the most popular for cooking. Their good melting qualities make them ideal for sauces, pasta and gratins. Blue cheeses lend real depth of flavour to dishes, and pungent ones such as Roquefort should be added sparingly. Soft rinded cheeses such as Brie and Camembert types are not often used in cooking because their large proportion of rind makes them wasteful. However, they are delicious melted on top of soups or bread and can also be grilled or baked while. Goat's cheese are increasingly popular and are very versatile – try them in salads, pizzas, sauces, stuffings and even desserts.

Cheese reacts differently depending on how it is cooked. The main principle is that it should not be exposed to too fierce a heat – except when grilling, in which case the cooking time should be brief. Overcooked cheese tends to be rubbery. Above a certain temperature the protein coagulates, separating the fat and water to produce a stringy texture. The secret is to add the cheese towards the end of cooking. If you are using it in a sauce, always take the pan off the heat and allow the cheese to melt in.

Hard cheeses can withstand higher temperatures than soft ones. Varieties such as haloumi, feta and mozzarella are best cooked quickly at high temperature. The classic example is mozzarella cooked in the blazing heat of a traditional pizza oven. The high fat or water content of soft cheeses means they blend easily with liquid, making them useful for vinaigrettes and other uncooked sauces (see the recipe for Goat's Cheese and Cumin Vinaigrette on page 20).

Finally, a couple of tips: when grating cheese, chill it first to firm it up as this makes the job easier. And take care when seasoning cheese dishes as most cheeses contain added salt – taste first.

cheese and your health

Cheese can make a valuable contribution to our diet, supplying generous amounts of protein, vitamin A and calcium, which helps prevent osteoporosis. It also contains vitamins B2, B12 and D, niacin and folic acid, as well as phosphorus and zinc. It is beneficial to children, because calcium aids the growth of strong bones and teeth, and also to the elderly, because it provides a concentration of nutrients that might otherwise be lacking in their diet. The vitamin B12 is especially welcome for vegetarians, who may like to seek out types made with a vegetarian rennet substitute rather than traditional rennet – a substance extracted from the stomach lining of calves to clot the milk.

There's no denying, however, that many cheeses are high in fat – a cause of dietary concern for most of us nowadays. But I do believe it's possible to enjoy cheese as part of a healthy diet. As in all things, moderation is the key. Set out to discover the wealth of artisan cheeses on offer and enjoy them just two or three times a week. This is more satisfying than consuming bland, plastic-wrapped, factory-produced cheeses on a daily basis. A lump of good farmhouse cheese, a hunk of bread and some salad make for a fulfilling meal and you won't need butter or any other form of fat with it.

In cooking, it really pays to use good-quality cheeses. If you add a farmhouse Cheddar to your cheese sauce rather than a factory one, for example, you will find the taste is so much stronger that you can get away with using less. The farmhouse version may be more expensive but you will save on both calories and cost.

Soft ripened cheeses such as Brie and Camembert are not as calorific as you might think, containing around two-thirds the fat of hard cheeses such as Cheddar and only half the fat of Stilton. And, of course, there are cheeses that are naturally low-fat, mainly the soft ones such as ricotta, fromage frais, cottage cheese and quark. You will find recipes for all of these in this book. But please, don't use the half-fat cheeses on sale in some supermarkets. These may have only half the fat but they have absolutely none of the flavour.

Several years ago, an irrational fear developed in Britain about the health risks of unpasteurized cheeses, which were wrongly seen as causing listeriosis. Since then, the government's Chief Medical Officer has completely exonerated unpasteurized cheeses, and, mercifully, they are just as safe to eat as pasteurized ones. However, there is a slight risk of listeriosis from rinded and mould-ripened cheeses (e.g. Camembert and Stilton), whether pasteurized or unpasteurized. Government advice is that these should be avoided by pregnant women, the very young, the very old, and anyone suffering from an immune-deficiency illness.

Typical Nutrition Values in Popular Cheeses Per 100g

Cheese	Carbs (g)	Fat (g)	Protein (g)	Calories (Kcal)
Brie	Trace	26.9	19.3	319
Camembert	Trace	23.7	20.9	297
Chaumes	1.0	25.4	21.0	317
Cheddar	0.1	34.4	25.5	410
Chèvre	Trace	25.6	21.0	314
Danish Blue	1.0	29.0	20.0	336
Dolcelatte	Trace	36.0	17.3	394
Edam	Trace	24.1	27.1	326
Feta	3.0	24.2	17.2	298
Fontina	0.1	30.45	25.2	381
Gorgonzola	Trace	26.0	19.0	333
Gouda	Trace	31.0	24.0	375
Gruyère	0.8	32.0	28.0	403
Mascarpone	4.8	40.30	5.5	404
Mozzarella (full-fat)	Trace	25.4	18.0	301
Mozzarella (half-fat)	1.8	10.5	20.0	182
Parmesan	Trace	32.7	39.4	452
Pont l'Évêque	Trace	22.5	24.0	299
Ricotta (full-fat)	2.6	14.8	10.0	185
Roquefort	1.8	29.0	21.0	352
Stilton	0.1	35.5	22.7	411

Notes on the Recipes

Butter is always unsalted.
Eggs are large free-range.
In white sauces, boiled milk is often specified. Although this is not essential, bringing the milk to the boil and then straining it before adding it to the sauce gives a smoother finish.

Alternative cheeses are suggested in most recipes. These are recommended replacements if the cheese in the ingredients list is hard to find, or Australian or American equivalents for readers in those countries. Occasionally, though, I have suggested a completely different cheese. This is to give a new twist to the existing recipe – for example, replacing the Cheddar in a soup with goat's cheese or Stilton. Feel free to experiment.

IMPORTANT

Some of the recipes contain raw or lightly cooked eggs, which may carry a slight risk of salmonella poisoning. These should be avoided by the very young, the very old, anyone suffering from an immune-deficiency illness, and pregnant women.

Because of the marginal risk of listeriosis, it is also advisable that these groups steer clear of rinded and mould-ripened cheeses.

basics

There are as many different recipes for vegetable stock as there are cooks, but most of them contain sweet-tasting vegetables such as carrots and leeks.

vegetable stock

MAKES ABOUT 1 LITRE

2 tablespoons olive oil
1 onion, chopped
1 small leek, chopped
75g celeriac, chopped
2 large carrots, chopped
1 celery stick, chopped
75g white cabbage, chopped
1/2 head fennel, chopped
4 garlic cloves, chopped
125ml white wine (optional)
4 black peppercorns
1 sprig of fresh thyme
1 bay leaf
1.5 litres water
2 teaspoons salt

Heat the oil in a large saucepan, add all the vegetables and the garlic and cook gently for about 5 minutes, until softened. Add the wine, if using, then add the peppercorns, thyme, bay leaf and water.

Bring to the boil, add the salt and simmer for 40 minutes, until reduced by a third of its original volume. Strain through a fine sieve and leave to cool. Refrigerate until required or freeze.

PG TIPS

You can buy chilled versions of fresh stock in supermarkets. These are generally of good quality and can be used in all the recipes requiring stock in this book. However, some of them are quite salty, so be careful when adding seasoning. Home-made stocks are, of course, considerably cheaper.

A light clear, refined chicken stock, ideal for sauces and soups.

chicken stock

MAKES ABOUT 1.75 LITRES

2.3kg raw chicken carcasses, or
  chicken wings and legs
350g onions, chopped
350g carrots, chopped
150g celery, chopped
1 leek, chopped
1 bouquet garni (see Tip)

Put the chicken carcasses in a large saucepan, cover with cold water and bring slowly to the boil. Skim off any impurities that rise to the surface, then add the vegetables and bouquet garni. Simmer very gently for 4 hours, then strain through a fine sieve and leave to cool. Refrigerate the stock until it is required or freeze.

PG TIPS

To make a bouquet garni, tie together 1 bay leaf and 2 sprigs each of fresh parsley and thyme and wrap in a small strip of green of leek.

This is ideal for using up those last pieces of cheese and rind that are left after grating as much as you can from a piece. Parmesan is perfect for this recipe. The cheese adds a wonderfully rich flavour to the stock, which can be used as a base for risottos, pastas, sauces and soups.

cheese-infused **chicken** stock

MAKES ABOUT 1 LITRE

15g unsalted butter
1 onion, sliced
1 leek, sliced
2 garlic cloves, peeled and halved
1 litre Chicken Stock
A few sprigs each of fresh parsley,
  rosemary & thyme
100g rinds of hard cheese

Heat the butter in a heavy-based pan, add the onion, leek and garlic and cook over a gentle heat until softened. Add the chicken stock, herbs and cheese rind and bring to the boil.

Reduce the heat and simmer for 20 minutes, then strain through a fine sieve and leave to cool. Refrigerate the stock until it is required or freeze.

You can use beef or veal bones to make this, but veal gives a better flavour.

meat stock

MAKES ABOUT 1.75 LITRES

90ml vegetable oil
900g beef or veal bones, chopped
  into small pieces
450g beef or veal trimmings, cut into
  small pieces
3 carrots, chopped
2 onions, chopped
1 celery stick, chopped
2 garlic cloves, crushed
50g tomato purée
1 bouquet garni (see Tip opposite)

Preheat the oven to 220ºC/425ºF/ gas 7. Heat half the oil in a roasting tin, add the bones and roast them for about 30 minutes, until well browned. Meanwhile, heat the remaining oil in a large, deep pan and fry the meat trimmings until very well browned.

Add the bones, vegetables and garlic to the pan, cover with water and bring slowly to the boil. Skim off any impurities that rise to the surface. Stir in the tomato purée and bouquet garni and simmer over a very low heat for 2 hours, skimming frequently. Strain through a fine sieve and leave to cool. Refrigerate until required or freeze.

reduced **meat** stock

Pour the strained meat stock into a pan and boil until reduced by half its volume. Store or freeze as above.

This is a classic white sauce that has been enriched with cream and egg and includes Gruyère cheese.

basic **cheese** sauce (cheese mornay)

MAKES ABOUT 600 ML

900ml milk
1 onion, peeled & studded with
 3–4 cloves
50g unsalted butter
50g plain flour
100g Gruyère, grated
1 teaspoon Dijon mustard
Freshly grated nutmeg
125ml double cream
2 egg yolks
Salt & freshly ground black pepper

Alternative cheeses
For an interestingly different sauce,
replace the Gruyère with a goat's
cheese or blue cheese

Put the milk and onion in a pan and bring to the boil, then remove from the heat and leave to stand for 5 minutes. Melt the butter in a separate pan and stir in the flour to make a roux. Cook gently, stirring, for 2–3 minutes.

Remove the onion from the milk and add the milk to the roux a little at a time, stirring constantly. Bring slowly to the boil, then reduce the heat and cook very gently for 20 minutes, stirring from time to time to prevent stirring.

Remove from the heat, add the cheese and stir until melted. Add the mustard and season with nutmeg, salt and pepper. If you like, strain through a fine sieve for a smoother sauce. Stir in the cream and egg yolks.

This sauce is simple to make and the result is both satisfying and tasty.

rapid **cheese** sauce

SERVES 4

125ml Vegetable Stock (see page 16)
125ml double cream
40g Parmesan, freshly grated
2 teaspoons arrowroot
75g chilled unsalted butter, cut into
 small pieces
Salt & freshly ground black pepper

Bring the vegetable stock and cream to the boil and boil for 2–3 minutes. Put the cheese and arrowroot in a bowl and mix to a paste with a little water. Add to the stock and stir over a gently heat until thickened. Whisk in the butter a few pieces at a time until smooth and creamy. Season to taste and serve straight away.

PG TIPS
To serve this sauce with fish, you can make it taste more interesting by adding fresh herbs such as chervil, chives and tarragon.

These can be prepared well ahead of time and stored in the fridge or even the freezer. You can then cut off slices to use as required – perhaps as a topping for grilled fish, steak or vegetables.

cheese butters

SERVE 4

camembert butter

MAKES ABOUT 190G

Camembert, rind removed
125g softened unsalted butter
Freshly ground black pepper

Process all the ingredients together in a blender or food processor, then scrape out on to a piece of foil. Shape into a log and roll up in the foil, then chill until required.

roquefort butter

MAKES ABOUT 250G

100g Roquefort
150g softened unsalted butter
1 tablespoon chopped fresh parsley

Prepare as for Camembert Butter.

roquefort & green peppercorn butter

Stir 1 tablespoon crushed green peppercorns into the Roquefort Butter.

ricotta, lemon thyme & garlic butter

MAKES 225G

100g ricotta
100g softened unsalted butter
1 garlic clove, crushed
1 tablespoon fresh lemon thyme
 leaves

Prepare as for Camembert Butter.

Throughout this book you will discover the versatility of this sauce. It is wonderful with fresh pasta and can also be used as a stuffing for vegetables, fish or chicken if you halve the amount of olive oil. You could also vary the herbs, replacing the coriander with basil, for example, or with a combination of fresh herbs.

coriander & **goat's cheese** pesto

MAKES ABOUT 300ML

1 garlic clove, crushed
50g fresh coriander leaves
1 tablespoon pine kernels
150ml extra-virgin olive oil
2 tablespoons freshly grated
  Parmesan
75g soft mild goat's cheese, such as
  Sainte-Maure, Golden Cross or
  Roubiliac
50g mascarpone
Salt & freshly ground black pepper

Alternative cheeses
Kervella (Aust), Montrachet (US) or
any other soft goat's cheese

Put the garlic, coriander and pine kernels in a blender and blitz to a purée, gradually adding the olive oil. Add the cheeses and blend again until the mixture has a thick, saucelike consistency. Season with salt and pepper.

This unusual vinaigrette can be served with spring vegetable salads and is also delicious with Carpaccio of Beef (see page 48) as an alternative to the dolcelatte mustard dressing.

goat's cheese & cumin vinaigrette

MAKES ABOUT 300ML

100g soft mild goat's cheese, such
  as Golden Cross
2 tablespoons hot water
2 tablespoons red wine vinegar
1/2 tablespoon ground cumin
1 tablespoon chopped fresh oregano
1 egg yolk
100ml vegetable oil or groundnut oil
Salt & freshly ground black pepper

Put the goat's cheese in a bowl, pour on the hot water and beat until smooth and creamy. Add the vinegar, cumin, oregano, if using, and egg yolk and whisk together until blended. Gradually whisk in the oil and then season to taste, being careful with the amount of salt you add as some goat's cheeses have a rather salty flavour.

Quark is extremely low in fat and so is very useful for anyone trying to reduce their fat intake – for whom mayonnaise would usually be out of bounds because of all the oil it contains. Although this recipe includes a little olive oil for flavour, most of it is replaced by quark, resulting in a healthier, more delicate mayonnaise.

quark mayonnaise

SERVES 4

2 egg yolks
2 tablespoons red wine vinegar
4 tablespoons olive oil
225g quark
2 tablespoons water
Salt & freshly ground black pepper

Alternative Cheeses
Low-fat fromage frais or ricotta

Whisk the egg yolks and vinegar with a pinch of salt until creamy. Whisk in the oil a little at a time, as if making mayonnaise, to form a light emulsion. Blend the quark with the water and add to the egg mixture, then season to taste with salt and pepper.

To make cheese pastry, add 3 tablespoons freshly grated Parmesan to the flour with the butter.

shortcrust pastry

MAKES 450G

250g plain flour
175g chilled unsalted butter,
  cut into small pieces
1 egg, beaten
A pinch of salt

Sift the flour on to a work surface or into a large bowl. Add the butter and blend together with your fingertips until it has a soft, sandy texture. Make a well in the centre and add the beaten egg and salt. Gently mix together with your fingertips to form a smooth, even dough. Wrap in cling film and chill for about 30 minutes or until required.

This rich pastry is suitable for most sweet tarts.

sweet pastry

MAKES 675G

350g plain flour
225g unsalted butter, cut into small
  pieces (at room temperature)
A pinch of salt
100g icing sugar, sifted
Finely grated zest of 1/2 lemon
1 egg, beaten

Sift the flour on to a work surface and make a well in the centre. Put the butter, salt, sugar and lemon zest in the well and then add the egg. With your fingertips, gradually bring the flour into the centre until all the ingredients come together to form a soft dough. Knead very lightly for 1 minute, until completely smooth, then form the dough into a ball. Wrap in cling film and chill for 2 hours.

This quick and easy brioche is great for breakfast but can also be used in both savoury and sweet dishes, such as Warm Brioche of Goat's Cheese with Mixed Leeks (see page 40) and Croque Mademoiselle (see page 178).

brioche

MAKES 12 BUNS OR 1 LOAF

10g fresh yeast
2 tablespoons milk
450g strong plain flour
1 teaspoon salt
20g caster sugar
4 eggs
100g softened unsalted butter
1 egg beaten with 1 tablespoon milk,
   to glaze

Dissolve the yeast in the milk. Sift the flour, salt and sugar on to a work surface and make a well in the centre. Beat the eggs with the yeast mixture, then pour them into the well in the flour. Gradually work the flour into the eggs with the heel of your hand until a soft dough is formed, then knead it for 2–3 minutes. Work in the softened butter, using the same method, and knead for about 10 minutes or until the dough has a smooth texture. It will feel slightly sticky to the touch. Cover with cling film and leave to rest in the refrigerator for 30 minutes.

Shape the dough into 12 balls and place in buttered individual brioche tins or shape into a loaf and place in a medium loaf tin. Cover and leave in a warm place for 30–40 minutes, until doubled in size. Preheat the oven to 200°C/300°F/gas 6.

Brush the brioche with the beaten egg and milk mixture and bake until golden brown – about 20 minutes for brioche buns, 40 minutes for a loaf. Turn out on to a wire rack to cool.

This loaf (see photograph on page 189) is very quick to make and it needs only one rising. Although most recipes tell you to use warm water when making bread, I find cold water works perfectly well. In fact it is probably safer, since if the water is too hot it may kill the yeast and prevent the loaf rising.

cheddar & onion loaf

MAKES 1 LOAF

1 heaped teaspoon fresh yeast
125ml water
2 teaspoons vegetable oil
275g strong plain flour
A pinch of salt
A pinch of sugar
1 egg, beaten
50g onion, finely diced
175g mature Cheddar, grated
25g Parmesan, freshly grated

Put the yeast in a small bowl, add the water and stir until the yeast has dissolved. Stir in the oil. Sift the flour, salt and sugar into a bowl and make a well in the centre. Pour in the yeast liquid and half the beaten egg and then stir in the flour to make a soft dough. Turn out on to a lightly floured work surface and knead for 8–10 minutes, until smooth and elastic. Leave to relax for about 2 minutes, until they are fully incorporated. Shape the dough into a loaf and place it in a greased 450g loaf tin. Cover with a damp tea towel and leave in a warm place for about 1 hour, until doubled in size.

Preheat the oven to 220°C/425°F/gas 7. Brush the top of the loaf with the remaining beaten egg and bake for 25–30 minutes, until the bread is golden brown and sounds hollow when turned out of the tin and tapped underneath. Turn out on to a wire rack to cool.

This is an excellent way of using up those tiny bits of crumbled Stilton or other blue cheeses. Colston Bassett Stilton is a true jewel in Britain's cheesemaking revival. It may seem extravagant to use it in a bread, but as the flavour is strong you don't need very much. (See photograph on page 189.)

stilton bread

MAKES 2 LOAVES

20g fresh yeast
300ml water
2 teaspoons malt extract
2 teaspoons golden syrup
500g strong plain flour
2 teaspoons salt
150g Colston Bassett Stilton,
  crumbled

Put the yeast in a small bowl, add a little of the water and stir to dissolve. Stir in the malt extract and golden syrup. Sift the flour and salt into a bowl and make a well in the centre. Pour in the yeast liquid and the remaining water and then stir in the flour to make a soft dough. Turn out on to a lightly floured work surface and knead for 8–10 minutes, until smooth and elastic. Return to the cleaned bowl, cover with a damp tea towel and leave in a warm place for about 50 minutes, until doubled in size.

Punch down the dough and divide it in half. Roll out each piece into a rectangle about 20 x 30cm. Sprinkle the Stilton evenly over the dough and roll up tightly. Place in 2 greased 450g loaf tins or shape into rounds and place on greased baking sheets. Cover with a damp tea towel and leave in a warm place, until risen. Preheat the oven to 200°C/400°F/gas 6. Sprinkle the loaves with a little flour and bake for 35–40 minutes, until the bread is golden brown on top and sounds hollow when turned out and tapped on the bottom.

Brioche dough is spread with mozzarella, olives and sun-dried tomatoes and then rolled up, producing an attractive and colourful spiral pattern when sliced. It's a wonderful bread to take on picnics.

italian picnic **loaf**

MAKES 1 LOAF

1 tablespoon olive oil
2 garlic cloves, crushed
50g sun-dried tomatoes in oil,
  drained & finely chopped
2 tablespoons chopped black olives
1 quantity of Brioche dough (see
  opposite)
1 ball of cow's milk mozzarella, well
  drained & cut into slices 5mm thick
Butter, for greasing
1 tablespoon freshly grated
  Parmesan
A little milk, for brushing

Heat half the olive oil in a small pan, add the garlic and cook gently for about 1 minute, until softened but not browned. Stir in the sun-dried tomatoes and olives and cook for 1 minute longer, then leave to cool.

Roll out the brioche dough into a 25cm square. Brush with the remaining olive oil, then arrange the mozzarella in overlapping slices over the top, starting 5cm in from the edge of the dough. Sprinkle over the olive and tomato mixture, then roll up the brioche tightly like a Swiss roll.

Lightly butter a large loaf tin and dust it with the grated Parmesan. Put the brioche roll in the tin, cover with a damp tea towel and leave in a warm place for 25 minutes, until risen and puffy. Preheat the oven to 200°C/400°F/gas 6. Brush the loaf with a little milk and then bake for 25 minutes, until it is golden brown on top and sounds hollow when turned out of the tin and tapped underneath. Serve warm.

chapter 1 **first courses**

My inclusion of cream cheese in this traditional Greek smoked fish purée would doubtless bring tears to the eyes of locals. I find it mellows and rounds the smoky flavour of the roe – try it and see what you think.

taramasalata with **cream cheese** on tapenade crostini

SERVES 4

3 slices of white bread,
 crusts removed
1 garlic clove, crushed
100g smoked cod's roe, skinned
75g cream cheese
3 tablespoons lemon juice
6 tablespoons olive oil
2 tablespoons tapenade
8 slices of crusty French bread,
 about 1cm thick
Salt & freshly ground black pepper

Soak the white bread in a little water or, better still, milk for 5 minutes. Squeeze out the excess moisture, then place the bread in a blender or food processor. Add the garlic, cod's roe and cream cheese and blitz to a smooth purée. Add the lemon juice and 4 tablespoons of the olive oil and blend again, then transfer to a bowl. Season to taste, then chill for at least 2 hours.

To serve, mix the tapenade with the remaining olive oil. Toast the French bread, spread it with the taramasalata and drizzle over the tapenade.

PG TIPS
Jars of tapenade, a black olive and anchovy paste, are readily available in supermarkets and delicatessens and the quality is usually quite good. Green olive tapenade works just as well. I like to serve these crostini with pre-dinner drinks or with a tipple of Ouzo. And why not?

The vibrant colours of this dish are almost as enticing as its robust flavours. Although I usually serve it warm, it is also very good cold. Substitute oregano or basil for the parsley, if you like.

twice-roasted red peppers with **haloumi,** capers & olives

SERVES 4

4 large red peppers
4 tablespoons olive oil
2 garlic cloves, thinly sliced
2 tablespoons chopped fresh
   flat-leaf parsley
12 black olives, stoned & halved
2 tablespoons superfine capers,
   rinsed & drained
8 slices of haloumi, 1cm thick
Salt & freshly ground black pepper

For the dressing
2 tablespoons white wine vinegar
125ml olive oil
1/4 teaspoon Dijon mustard
1/2 small red chilli, deseeded &
   finely chopped

Alternative cheese
Feta

Preheat the oven to 200°C, 400°F, gas 6. Cut the peppers in half lengthways, brush with a little of the olive oil and season with salt and pepper. Bake for 1 hour or until tender. Remove from the oven and leave until cool enough to handle, then peel off the skin and cut the peppers lengthways into strips 2cm wide.

Lightly brush a gratin dish with olive oil. Put the pepper strips in it, sprinkle over the garlic, parsley, olives and capers and season with salt and pepper. Lay the haloumi cheese slices on top, drizzle over the remaining olive oil and return to the oven for 10–12 minutes, until the cheese is just starting to melt.

Meanwhile, whisk together all the ingredients for the dressing and season to taste. Remove the peppers from the oven and drizzle over the dressing. Serve warm, with herb-grilled crusty bread (see Tip below).

PG TIPS
To make herb-grilled crusty bread, brush slices of baguette with olive oil and sprinkle with chopped fresh herbs, then put under a hot grill until golden.

This is my version of the Greek dish ktipiti, which is usually a dip rather than a mousse. The saltiness of the feta cheese contrasts well with the peppery rocket.

feta & roasted pepper mousse with rocket & pine kernels

SERVES 4

1 large red pepper
150ml olive oil
225g Greek feta
200g Greek yogurt
1 garlic clove, crushed
3 gelatine leaves
1 tablespoon balsamic vinegar
A handful of young rocket leaves
1 tablespoon pine kernels
Salt & freshly ground black pepper

Preheat the oven to 200°C, 400°F, gas 6. Rub the pepper with 2 tablespoons of the olive oil, place on a baking tray and bake for 40 minutes or until tender. Leave until cool enough to handle, then peel off the skin, cut the pepper in half and remove the seeds. Put the pepper in a blender with the feta, yogurt, garlic and 4 tablespoons of the olive oil and blitz to a fine purée.

Put the gelatine in a small pan, cover with about 3 tablespoons of water and leave for 5 minutes to soften. Melt over a gentle heat until clear. Stir it thoroughly into the purée and strain the mixture through a fine sieve. Season to taste and pour into 4 ramekin dishes or coffee cups. Chill for 1–2 hours, until set.

Whisk together the balsamic vinegar and the remaining olive oil to make a dressing and season to taste with salt and pepper. Unmould the mousses on to individual serving plates. Toss the rocket and pine kernels with the dressing and arrange them around the mousses.

Corniottes are little triangular pastries which can be filled with sweet or savoury ingredients. Baked until crisp, they are a speciality of Burgundy, where they are served as a snack. If you don't have any Marc de Bourgogne, you could use kirsch instead.

emmenthal corniottes with marc de bourgogne

MAKES ABOUT 20

250g fromage blanc or cream cheese
150ml crème fraîche
2 tablespoons Marc de Bourgogne
200g Emmenthal, grated
2 eggs, beaten
Freshly grated nutmeg
1 quantity of shortcrust pastry (see page 21)
1 egg beaten with 2 tablespoons milk, to glaze
Salt & freshly ground black pepper

Alternative cheeses
Swiss Appenzell or Gruyère

Preheat the oven to 200°C, 400°F, gas 6. Put the fromage blanc or cream cheese, crème fraîche and Marc de Bourgogne in a bowl and beat in the grated Emmenthal and eggs to form a paste. Season with nutmeg, salt and pepper and set aside.

Roll out the pastry until it is 3mm thick and cut out 10cm rounds – you should have about 20. Put some filling in the centre of each one, brush the edges with a little cold water and then pull 3 sides of the pastry up over the filling to form a point. Pinch together firmly to seal. Chill for up to 1 hour, then brush with the beaten egg and milk mixture and bake for 20–25 minutes, until golden. Serve hot or warm.

PG TIPS
Smaller corniottes make great cocktail canapés. They also freeze successfully, so they can be prepared in advance and baked straight from the freezer when required. Puff pastry works just as well as shortcrust pastry.

I love the textures of this warm smoked salmon and blue cheese salad, the salmon delicate and meltingly tender, while the creamy mild-tasting Cornish blue is an excellent contrast to the dressing.

seared smoked salmon & **cornish blue** salad

SERVES 4

200g mixed salad leaves
1 medium carrot, finely shredded
175g red cherry tomatoes, halved
4 tablespoons French dressing
 (of your choice)
120g Cornish blue cheese, crumbled
2 tablespoons mild olive oil
450g cleaned smoked salmon,
 cut into 1cm thick slices
2 cooked beetroots, cut into wedges
Small handful of fresh mint leaves
Salt & freshly ground black pepper

Place the salad leaves, carrot, tomato and 3 tablespoons of the dressing in a bowl and toss together. Add half the Cornish blue cheese and season to taste. Divide the salad between 4 individual serving dishes.

Heat the oil in a non-stick frying pan, and when hot add the smoked salmon slices and quickly flash-fry for 10 seconds on each side, then remove and keep warm until you are ready to serve.

Divide the salmon between the 4 dishes and add the beetroot wedges. Sprinkle over the remaining cheese, drizzle with the remaining dressing, scatter with mint leaves and serve immediately.

The combination of oysters and blue cheese may sound unexpected but it is a marriage made in culinary heaven. This is my version of a dish I came across at the Bel-Air Hotel in Los Angeles, during a week I spent there as guest chef. The original recipe used Maytag Blue, a creamy, salty cheese from Iowa, but I have substituted Bleu d'Auvergne.

glazed oysters on crushed potatoes with parsley & **bleu d'auvergne**

SERVES 4

250g new potatoes
4 tablespoons milk
4 tablespoons olive oil
2 tablespoons chopped fresh flat-
  leaf parsley
24 plump oysters
Salt & freshly ground black pepper

For the sauce
2 egg yolks
4 tablespoons dry white wine
150ml double cream
75g Bleu d'Auvergne, crumbled

Alternative cheeses
Roquefort, Maytag Blue (US) or
  Oregon Blue (US) or Bellingham
  Blue (IRE)

Cook the potatoes in boiling salted water until just tender, then drain well. Place in a bowl, add the milk, olive oil and parsley and crush them coarsely with a fork. Season with salt and pepper and keep warm.

Open the oysters and remove from the shells, reserving the juices (see Tip below). Discard the top part of each shell and clean the bottom part.

For the sauce, whisk the egg yolks and wine together in a small bowl, then set the bowl over a pan of simmering water and whisk until the mixture thickens and doubles in volume. Boil the cream and cheese together for 2–3 minutes, then fold into the whisked egg yolk and wine mixture along with the strained oyster juices.

To serve, divide the crushed potatoes between the cleaned oyster shells. Season the oysters, put them on top of the potato mixture and then coat with the sauce. Place under a hot grill for 5 minutes, until golden (or place in a hot oven). Serve immediately.

PG TIPS
To open oysters you need an oyster knife or a short, strong-bladed knife.

Wrap your hand in a tea towel to protect it, then take hold of an oyster and insert the knife blade between the shells, next to the hinge. Twist the knife to lever open the top shell, then cut the muscle connecting the oyster to the shell. Next, loosen the muscle connecting the oyster to the bottom shell. Take out the oyster and strain the juices into a bowl.

This simple recipe is a savoury version of French toast. A good aged Taleggio cheese adds a creamy, aromatic and slightly sour flavour, which partners the sweetness of the tomatoes and brioche well. If yellow plum tomatoes are available, why not use half red, half yellow? The colours look stunning.

parmesan brioche toast with **taleggio**, sautéed plum tomatoes & oregano

SERVES 4

2 tablespoons olive oil
2 garlic cloves, crushed
450g small plum tomatoes,
  halved
2 tablespoons chopped fresh
  oregano
2 eggs, beaten
100ml milk
50g Parmesan, freshly
  grated
Freshly grated nutmeg
4 slices of brioche (see page 22), cut
  2cm thick
40g unsalted butter
4 tablespoons aged Taleggio slivers
Salt & freshly ground black pepper

Alternative cheeses
Substitute freshly shaved Parmesan
or Asiago for the Taleggio

Heat the oil in a pan, add the garlic and cook for 1 minute. Add the tomatoes and sauté them until they begin to soften. Season with salt and pepper and stir in the oregano. Keep warm.

In a shallow bowl, whisk together the eggs, milk and Parmesan cheese, seasoning with a little nutmeg, salt and pepper. Cut the brioche slices into rounds, if liked, or leave them whole. Dip them in the egg mixture on both sides. Heat the butter in a frying pan, add the brioche and cook for 2–3 minutes on each side, until golden.

Put the Parmesan French toasts on serving plates and arrange the tomatoes on top. Scatter over the Taleggio and place under a hot grill to melt the cheese slightly before serving.

PG TIPS
It's important to use good, sweet, ripe tomatoes here. Plum tomatoes are generally fuller flavoured, but if they are not readily available, try using the larger, rounded varieties, sliced. Add a pinch of sugar if their flavour is not all it should be. White rolls or muffins can be substituted for the brioche.

Although buffalo mozzarella is generally held to be superior to cow's milk mozzarella, in this recipe I actually prefer to use the cow's milk cheese because it is less milky in texture and holds its shape better.

ratatouille-stuffed **mozzarella** wrapped in prosciutto

SERVES 4

3 tablespoons extra-virgin olive oil
1 small aubergine, sliced
1 courgette, sliced
1 garlic clove, crushed
1 teaspoon chopped fresh thyme
2 balls of cow's milk mozzarella
2 plum tomatoes, skinned & sliced
8 thin slices of prosciutto
50g unsalted butter
Salt & freshly ground black pepper

For the dressing
2 tablespoons balsamic vinegar
6 tablespoons extra-virgin olive
 oil
1 tomato, skinned, deseeded & diced
1/2 tablespoon chopped black olives
6 fresh basil leaves, shredded

Alternative cheese
Provolone

To make the ratatouille, heat the oil in a frying pan and fry the aubergine and courgette slices until tender. Stir in the garlic and thyme and cook for 1 minute, then season and leave to cool.

Cut each mozzarella horizontally into 4 equal slices and season lightly. Cover 4 slices with layers of aubergine, courgette and tomato, then top with the remaining cheese slices, making 4 ratatouille-stuffed mozzarella sandwiches in all. Wrap each one in 2 slices of prosciutto to secure the filling and chill for at least 30 minutes.

Heat the butter in a large frying pan, add the cheese sandwiches and fry until golden, about 2–3 minutes on each side. Place on 4 serving plates. Mix together all the ingredients for the dressing and season to taste. Pour it over the cheese sandwiches and serve straight away.

PG TIPS
Try grilling the stuffed mozzarella on a barbecue for a superb smoky flavour. Some people may be surprised to see that I do not advise salting the aubergine in this recipe. When slicing aubergines thinly, I really see little point in the exercise. However, when I use them in halves, I do usually salt them before cooking.

Moutabel is a Middle Eastern dish of puréed aubergine and tahini, also known as baba ghanoush. I find aubergines have a great affinity with cheese. In this dish, aubergine halves are stuffed with a moutabel-style filling and then topped with goat's cheese and thyme. Serve on salad leaves with a dressing of Middle Eastern flavours, such as a vinaigrette containing peeled, deseeded and finely diced tomato, chopped coriander and a little ground cumin.

roasted aubergine moutabel with **roubiliac** & thyme

SERVES 4

3 medium aubergines
2 tablespoons tahini
1 garlic clove, crushed
1 teaspoon ground cumin
2 tablespoons lemon juice
1 Roubiliac goat's cheese log, cut into 12 slices
2 tablespoons fresh thyme leaves
4 tablespoons walnut oil
Salt & freshly ground black pepper

Alternative cheese
Any soft fresh goat's cheese like Kervella (AUS), Coachfarm Goat (USA) or St Tola (IRE)

Preheat the oven to 190°C, 375°F, gas 5. Cut the aubergines in half, score the cut sides with a knife in a criss-cross pattern and bake for 45 minutes–1 hour, until tender. The exterior should be slightly charred but not burnt. Remove from the oven and leave to cool, then scoop out the flesh without damaging the skins. Chop the flesh very finely and mix it with the tahini, garlic, cumin, lemon juice and some salt and pepper.

Refill the aubergine skins with this mixture (there may only be enough to fill 4 halves), retaining the original shape of the aubergines. Put them in a lightly oiled, shallow ovenproof dish. Top each one with the slices of goat's cheese, sprinkle over the thyme leaves and drizzle with the walnut oil. Return to the oven for 8–10 minutes, until the cheese is golden and just beginning to melt. Cool slightly before serving.

This dish of simply fried sheep's milk cheese is served as a staple in tavernas throughout the Greek islands. Its beauty lies in its simplicity. It must be one of the easiest dishes to prepare, with just three ingredients, but it is delicious – and exceedingly moreish.

saganaki (fried sheep's cheese with lemon)

SERVES 4

75g unsalted butter
8 slices of kasseri/kefalotiri, 2cm thick
Juice of 3/4 lemon
Salt & freshly ground black pepper

Alternative cheese
Haloumi

Heat the butter in a large frying pan until foaming, add the cheese slices and fry for 1–2 minutes on each side, until golden. Season lightly with salt and pepper and then pour the lemon juice over the cheese in the pan. Serve straight away, with lots of crusty bread.

PG TIPS
The lemon juice nicely flavours the butter, but to add an extra dimension I occasionally like to add fresh capers and herbs. In Greece the cheese is sometimes flamed with brandy at the table.

Like flamiche (see page 41), goyère is a rich cheese tart from Belgium and northern France. Some recipes specify a pastry base while others use a bread dough, similar to that of a pizza. Here I give my favourite version, which has a yeasted dough for the base. The filling for goyère is generally made with a pungent – or, frankly, smelly – rindwashed cheese such as Maroilles or Livarot. Not for the faint-hearted, but when mixed with smoked bacon and potatoes it makes a wonderfully flavoured dish.

goyère

SERVES 4–6

450g potatoes, cut into small cubes
25g unsalted butter
1 small onion, finely chopped
100g smoked bacon, chopped
125g Maroilles, rind removed, cut into 5mm dice
2 eggs, beaten
100ml crème fraîche or double cream
Salt & freshly ground black pepper

For the base
75g unsalted butter
3 tablespoons milk
15g fresh yeast
225g strong plain flour
2 eggs, beaten
A pinch of salt
A pinch of brown sugar

Alternative cheese
Connoisseurs should look out for an interesting English cheese called Stinking Bishop. The rind is washed with the pear variety of the same name, also used to make perry or pear cider, which gives the cheese its strong-smelling yet creamy-tasting character

For the base, warm the butter and milk over a low heat until the butter has just melted. Leave until tepid, then stir in the yeast until dissolved. Sift the flour into a bowl, make a well in the centre and add the beaten eggs, salt and brown sugar. Add the yeast mixture to the eggs and mix in the flour to give a smooth dough. Turn the dough out on to a lightly floured work surface and knead for 5 minutes or until smooth. Return it to the cleaned bowl, cover with a damp cloth and leave in a warm place until doubled in size.

For the filling, cook the potatoes in boiling salted water until just tender, then drain well. Heat the butter in a pan, add the onion and cook over a gentle heat until soft but not coloured. Add the bacon and cook for 5 minutes, then remove from the heat and leave to cool.

Put the potatoes, onion, bacon and cheese in a bowl and mix in the eggs and crème fraîche or cream. Season to taste with salt and pepper.

Knock back the risen dough and roll out until it is 5mm thick. Use to line a 23cm flan ring, leaving a good amount of dough overlapping the edge. Place on a baking sheet, fill with the potato, bacon and cheese mixture and leave in a warm place to rise for 30 minutes, until the dough is puffy. Preheat the oven to 170°C, 325°F, gas 3.

Trim off the excess dough, then bake the tart in the oven for 45 minutes–1 hour, until golden and set.

Ripe, sweet pears make an excellent foil for the sharp blue cheese and the aromatic rosemary. As an alternative dish, try replacing the pear and Beenleigh Blue with slices of mozzarella and tomato, top them with a covering of pesto and bake the galettes as usual.

pear, **beenleigh blue** & rosemary galettes

SERVES 4

2 small egg whites
250g Beenleigh Blue
1 tablespoon crème fraîche
1 quantity of shortcrust pastry
  (see page 21)
1 tablespoon finely chopped
  fresh rosemary, plus a few
  leaves to garnish
50g unsalted butter, plus a little
  melted butter for brushing
2 large, ripe but firm pears, peeled,
  cored & cut into slices 1cm thick
1 tablespoon caster sugar
1 teaspoon cumin seeds
2 egg yolks, beaten with
  1 tablespoon milk, to glaze
Salt & freshly ground black pepper

Alternative cheeses
A fairly sharp blue cheese is needed,
such as Gorgonzola, Roquefort,
Buxton Blue or Oxford Blue

Whisk the egg whites until just frothy. Put the cheese in a bowl and crush it lightly with a fork, then add the egg whites and crème fraîche and mix to a coarse paste. Season with salt and pepper, then chill.

Roll out the pastry to about 3mm thick. Using a plain or fluted cutter, cut out four 12cm circles. Put them on a baking sheet and prick well all over with a fork to prevent them rising too much in the oven. Carefully spread the cheese mixture over the pastry rounds, leaving a 1–2cm border, then sprinkle with the chopped rosemary and place in the refrigerator.

Preheat the oven to 200°C, 400°F, gas 6. Melt the butter in a shallow pan, then add the pear slices, sugar and enough water to form a light syrup around the pears – about 3 tablespoons. Cook gently for 6–8 minutes, until the pears are tender, then leave to cool.

Arrange the pear slices on top of the galettes in neatly overlapping circles and brush with a little melted butter. Sprinkle over the cumin seeds and a few rosemary leaves, season with salt and pepper and bring up the edges of the pastry over the pears to form a crust. Brush the pastry all over with the beaten egg yolks and bake for 15–20 minutes or until golden. Cool the galettes slightly before serving.

PG TIPS
The galettes can be assembled several hours in advance – or even the night before – and chilled until you are ready to bake them. If you prefer, you can substitute puff pastry for the shortcrust.

I first prepared this brioche for a private party of eight vegetarians in the Lanesborough's Conservatory restaurant, as part of a seven-course gastronomic vegetarian menu. It was voted the star of the show and now makes regular appearances on my menu.

warm brioche of **goat's cheese** with minted leeks

SERVES 4

50g unsalted butter
2 young leeks, thinly sliced
1 tablespoon chopped fresh mint
Freshly grated nutmeg
4 brioche buns, 5cm in diameter
 (see page 22)
4 crottin de Chavignol goat's
 cheeses, cut horizontally in half
Salt & freshly ground black pepper

Alternative cheeses
A good English alternative is a well-aged Chabis, produced in East Sussex on the same farm as Golden Cross. Or you could use 4 slices of Sainte-Maure goat's cheese, cut 2.5cm thick

Preheat the oven to 200°C, 400°F, gas 6. Melt the butter in a pan, add the leeks and cook over a low heat for 8–10 minutes or until tender. You may need to add a little water if the leeks become too dry and stick to the pan. Remove from the pan and stir in the mint, then season to taste with nutmeg, salt and pepper.

Cut a 1cm slice off the top of each brioche and set aside, then carefully hollow out the centre of each bun. Fill with the minted leeks. Top the leeks with the goat's cheese and then put the brioches in the oven for 5 minutes to heat through. The cheese should just be starting to melt. Replace the brioche tops and serve immediately.

PG TIPS
Try topping the cheese with a little basil pesto before putting the brioches in the oven. I much prefer to prepare fresh pesto, which can be made in minutes in a blender. Shop-bought pesto is fine, but nothing quite matches the flavour and aroma of fresh basil. Filo pastry makes a good substitute for the brioche: simply top the leeks with the cheese and wrap well in the filo, then bake until golden.

Here's a Norwegian take on the Mexican dish. It makes a great starter or hearty snack. Serve with fresh tomato salsa and plenty of sour cream.

mediterranean tortillas with **jarlsberg**

SERVES 4

4 tablespoons olive oil
1 small aubergine, trimmed and
  thinly sliced
1 red pepper, halved, deseeded and
  cut into strips 1cm wide
175g sunblush tomatoes in oil,
  drained
1 red chilli, halved, seeded and
  finely chopped
3 tablespoons fresh coriander,
  roughly chopped
225g Jarlsberg, freshly grated
8 large tortillas
100g tomato salsa
100ml sour cream

Heat a large frying pan and add 3 tablespoons of oil. Add the aubergine, pepper, tomatoes and chilli and stir-fry for 8-10 minutes, until tender. Remove from the heat. Add the coriander and cheese and let it melt.

Lightly grease another frying pan with the remaining oil. Lay a tortilla flat in the pan and top with a quarter of the vegetables and cheese mix. Top with the second tortilla and press down gently. Cook over a medium heat until the bottom of the tortilla is golden and crisp – about 2 minutes.

Cover with a plate and turn the pan over to lift out the tortilla. Slide it back into the pan and brown the other side. Repeat with the remaining tortillas and filling. Cut into triangles and serve immediately with tomato salsa and sour cream.

I got the idea for this recipe from Pierre Carrier, the proprietor of the Hotel Albert Premier in Chamonix, France. His version used a local Reblochon made of goat's milk, which is well worth buying if you ever happen to see it. Although the dish is fairly expensive to make, the flavours are out of this world. Serve as a substantial first course or a delicious and unusual lunch dish.

baked **reblochon** in savoy cabbage

SERVES 4

3 tablespoons vegetable oil
100g potatoes, cut into 5mm cubes
1 onion, finely chopped
75g smoked bacon, cut into lardons
 (small strips)
50g chanterelle mushrooms,
 thinly sliced
75g button mushrooms, thinly sliced
2 tablespoons chopped fresh chives
8 green cabbage leaves, such as
 Savoy or Primo
Freshly grated nutmeg
1 Reblochon, rind removed
25g unsalted butter, melted
300ml Reduced Meat Stock
 (see page 17)
Salt & freshly ground black pepper

Alternative cheeses
Baby Saint-Nectaire, Pont-l'Évêque,
a plain or smoked Gubbeen,
Polkobin (AUS) or Jindi Brie (AUS)

Heat 1 tablespoon of the oil in a frying pan and sauté the potatoes until golden brown and just tender. Remove from the pan and set aside. Add the remaining oil to the pan and stir in the onion, bacon and both types of mushroom. Raise the heat and cook until golden and tender. Add to the potatoes, stir in the chives and leave to cool.

Preheat the oven to 200°C, 400°F, gas 6. Trim the cabbage leaves and cook them in boiling salted water until just tender. Remove with a slotted spoon and refresh in cold running water, then drain well and dry on a cloth. Lay out the leaves, slightly overlapping, on a work surface and season with nutmeg, salt and pepper.

Slice the Reblochon in half horizontally, cover one half with the potato mixture and top with the other half to form a sandwich. Place the Reblochon in the centre of the cabbage leaves and fold them over to cover the cheese completely. Season again and brush with the melted butter. Place in a baking dish and bake for about 12–15 minutes, until thoroughly heated through. Meanwhile, heat the reduced meat stock. When ready, transfer the cheese to a serving dish and pour the meat stock around it. Serve cut into wedges.

PG TIPS
Try wrapping the cheese in puff pastry rather than cabbage leaves. Swiss chard or spinach could easily replace the cabbage, if preferred. For vegetarians, the meat stock can be substituted with red wine vinegar or walnut oil dressing.

You need kasseri cheese for this recipe, a mild, creamy sheep's milk cheese which is now available from some Greek delicatessens. The artichokes are filled with a tangy cheese and herb mixture, which also makes a very good stuffing for tomatoes and aubergines.

greek-style baked artichokes with coriander, mint & lemon

SERVES 4

8 medium or 4 large globe
  artichokes
Juice & zest of 1 lemon
50g fresh white breadcrumbs
2 garlic cloves, crushed
1 tablespoon chopped fresh mint
1 tablespoon chopped fresh
  coriander
50g kasseri, grated
150ml olive oil
75g feta, crumbled
150ml dry white wine
Salt & freshly ground black pepper

Alternative cheeses
There is an American version of
kasseri from Wisconsin, made with
cow's milk and tasting a little
sharper and saltier. Italian
provolone could be used instead

Preheat the oven to 180°C, 350°F, gas 4. To prepare the artichokes, snap off the stalks and trim away the dark, fibrous outer leaves until you reach the tender, inner green leaves, rubbing the artichokes with the lemon juice as you go to prevent discoloration. Slice off about one third from the top of each artichoke. Carefully remove the hairy inner choke with a teaspoon. Drop the artichokes into a bowl of water acidulated with lemon juice.

In a bowl, mix together the lemon zest, breadcrumbs, garlic, mint, coriander, grated kasseri and 2 tablespoons of the olive oil. Season with salt and pepper.

Drain and dry the artichokes, then fill them with the feta. Top with the stuffing mixture. Place them in a baking dish, sprinkle over the white wine and the remaining oil and top up with water until the liquid reaches halfway up the sides of the artichokes. Bake for 35 minutes or until tender, basting frequently, then put the artichokes under a hot grill for a few minutes to brown the stuffing. Serve hot or cold.

My good friend Stuart Partridge, chef at the Hassler Hotel in Rome, first prepared this dish during a recent visit to the Lanesborough. I love the pure simplicity of its flavours. You could serve the courgettes with a tomato sauce but I like them best with just a squeeze of lemon juice. Although very young courgettes with their yellow flowers still attached are sold in markets in France and Italy, they are not generally available in the UK. However, if you grow your own courgettes, you can pick them for this recipe when they are just the right size.

crisp, flowering courgettes with **mozzarella** & anchovy

SERVES 4

8 courgettes, about 5cm long,
  with flowers still attached
4 tinned anchovy fillets
1 ball of cow's milk mozzarella
3 tablespoons Chinese flour
  (see Tip)
Vegetable oil for deep-frying
Salt & freshly ground black pepper
Sprigs of fresh flat-leaf parsley, to
  garnish
Lemon wedges, to serve

Trim about 1cm off the end of each courgette and discard (or save for another use). Carefully wipe clean the courgette flowers and remove the stamen from the centre of each one. Soak the anchovy fillets in water for 10 minutes, then dry them on kitchen paper. Cut each anchovy fillet in half. Cut the mozzarella into 8 batons approximately the size of your index finger. Place a piece of anchovy on each mozzarella baton, then place inside the courgette flowers and twist the ends of the blossoms to secure the filling.

Mix the Chinese flour with enough water to make a thin batter; it should coat the back of a spoon. Heat the oil in a deep-fat fryer or large saucepan to 180°C, 350°F. Dip the stuffed courgettes in the batter and deep-fry them for 1–2 minutes, until crisp and golden, turning them occasionally. Drain them thoroughly on kitchen paper. Quickly drop the sprigs of parsley into the hot oil and fry for about 10 seconds, until crisp, then drain on kitchen paper. Serve the courgettes immediately, garnished with the deep-fried parsley and accompanied by lemon wedges.

PG TIPS
Chinese flour is available in oriental food shops, but if you can't find any, make a tempura batter instead. Put 1 small egg yolk and 125ml iced water in a bowl, then gently mix in 125g plain flour and a pinch of salt; it should be slightly lumpy. Dip the stuffed courgettes in the batter and proceed as above. If you are keen to try this recipe but can't track down courgette flowers, wrap the cheese and anchovy in blanched spinach or roll in sautéed thin slices of aubergine before frying.

This savoury French toast is made with Emmenthal one of the great classic chesses. It is one of my favourite dishes for a real breakfast treat or light brunch option.

emmenthal 'french toast' with asparagus & poached egg

SERVES 4

45g unsalted butter
2 tablespoons chopped fresh chives
8 slices of good quality white bread, crusts removed
150g Emmenthal cheese, thinly sliced
2 eggs, beaten
4 tablespoons milk
2 tablespoons freshly grated Parmesan reggianno
2 tablespoons double, whipping cream
Freshly grated nutmeg
2 tablespoons olive oil
1 tablespoon white wine vinegar
4 eggs
8 tender, green aspaprgus tips, peeled
Salt & freshly ground black pepper

In a bowl, cream 25g butter with the chopped chives and a little salt and pepper. Butter all the slices of the bread on one side, then place Emmental cheese on 4 of them. Top with the remaining buttered slices to make 4 sandwiches.

In a dish, whisk together the eggs, milk, cream and parmesan, salt, pepper and a little pinch of nutmeg. Pass the 4 sandwiches through the egg mixture, ensuring the mixture is soaked into the bread.

Meanwhile, heat a large non-stick pan with the olive oil. When it is moderately hot, add a sandwich to the pan. Cook for 1–2 minutes on each side, until golden. Repeat with the other 3 sandwiches. You can do this in one motion so that you soak each sandwich, then transfer it to the pan, one at a time.

Meanwhile, bring 2 separate pans of water to the boil, add the vinegar to one pan and reduce to a simmer. Carefully crack the eggs into the pan and poach for 2–3 minutes until set, but still soft in the centre. (You may have to do this in two gos.) Remove and drain the eggs on a cloth and some kitchen paper. Cook the asparagus tips in the other boiling water. Remove and drain, season with salt and pepper and finish with the remaining butter.

To serve, cut the French toasts in half diagonally, place 2 French toast halves on each serving plate. Top with the asparagus tips and a poached egg. Serve immediately.

This mustard and blue cheese dressing makes a good alternative to the olive oil and Parmesan cheese that normally accompany carpaccio of beef. To make a warm carpaccio, use thin steaks – about 5mm thick – and grill over a charcoal grill for about 1 minute per side.

carpaccio of beef with **dolcelatte** mustard dressing

SERVES 4

450g beef fillet
4 tablespoons olive oil
2 tablespoons coarse sea salt
300g celeriac
Juice of ½ lemon
3 tablespoons walnut oil
225g cornsalad (or mixed salad
   leaves)
Salt & freshly ground black pepper

For the dressing
1 egg yolk
2 tablespoons Dijon mustard
1 tablespoon white wine vinegar
1 teaspoon soft brown sugar
5 tablespoons vegetable oil
1 tablespoon finely chopped fresh
   dill, plus a few sprigs to garnish
50g dolcelatte

Alternative cheeses
Dunsyre Blue, Danish Blue, Blue
Castello (AUS), Dorset Blue or
Yorkshire Blue

Cut the beef fillet into wafer-thin slices across the grain. If you find it difficult to slice the meat this thinly, cut thicker slices, place them between 2 sheets of oiled cling film and beat out carefully with a rolling pin or meat mallet. Spread the slices in a single layer over 4 large serving plates. Sprinkle with the olive oil, coarse salt and some freshly ground black pepper.

For the dressing, put the egg yolk in a bowl and whisk in the mustard, vinegar and sugar. Gradually add the oil in a thin stream, whisking all the time, as if making mayonnaise. Stir in the chopped dill. Put the dolcelatte in a separate bowl, pour on 2 tablespoons of boiling water and mix to a smooth paste. Add this paste to the dressing, blending it in well. Adjust the seasoning carefully as the dolcelatte will be quite salty.

Peel the celeriac, then grate it coarsely or cut it into fine strips (a mandolin is useful for this). Put it in a bowl, toss with the lemon juice and walnut oil and season to taste.

To serve, toss the cornsalad with the dressing and arrange on top of the beef, then sprinkle over the celeriac. Garnish with sprigs of dill.

PG TIPS
Chill the beef briefly in the freezer to make it easier to slice. If the prospect of slicing and salting the beef seems daunting, try using a cured meat such as Bresaola or even Parma ham – they both work well. The crisp, nutty texture of the celeriac lends a special flavour to the dish. Make every effort to get hold of some; you will not be disappointed!

chapter 2 **soups**

Some people are quite purist about what should go in a vichysoisse, which traditionally is made with leek and potato, but I think this version is definitely worthy of consideration. Intense yet delicate in flavour, it makes an ideal soup for early autumn. Like the original, it's thickened with cream and served chilled, garnished with chives.

pear, celeriac & **stilton** vichysoisse

SERVES 4

25g unsalted butter
1 onion, finely diced
300g celeriac, peeled & finely diced
2 ripe pears, peeled, cored & finely diced
1 litre Chicken Stock (see page 16) or Vegetable Stock (see page 16)
750ml single cream
75g Stilton, crumbled
2 tablespoons chopped fresh chives
Salt & freshly ground black pepper

Alternative cheeses
Shropshire Blue, dolcelatte, Milawa Blue (AUS), Gippsland Tarago River Blue (AUS) or Oregon Blue (US)

Heat the butter in a pan, add the onion and celeriac and cook over a gentle heat until they begin to soften, about 8–10 minutes. Stir in the pears and cook for 3–4 minutes. Add the stock and bring to the boil, then reduce the heat and simmer for 25 minutes, until the vegetables are tender. Remove from the heat, stir in the cream and Stilton and then purée the soup in a blender until smooth. Leave to cool, then chill thoroughly.

Before serving it may be necessary to thin down the soup with a little milk, stock or cream. Stir in the chives and season to taste.

PG TIPS
I'm often asked what is the correct consistency for puréed soups. In my experience, a good general rule is that they should be approximately the consistency of single cream, that is thick enough to coat the back of a spoon.

These cloud-like cheese meringues not only taste great but also make a lovely presentation for this delicate, peppery-tasting pea soup.

pea & watercress soup with **emmenthal** floating islands

SERVES 4

50g unsalted butter
50g onion, roughly chopped
1 leek, roughly chopped
1 litre Chicken Stock (see page 16)
450g shelled fresh or frozen peas
2 bunches of watercress, tough
  stalks removed
2 egg whites
75g Emmenthal cheese, freshly
  grated, plus extra to serve
600ml milk
150ml double cream
Salt & freshly ground black pepper

Heat the butter in a heavy-based pan, add the onion and leek and cook gently for 4–5 minutes, until softened. Add the stock and bring to the boil. Add the peas and simmer until tender – the cooking time will depend on whether you are using fresh or frozen peas. Stir in the watercress, then pour the soup into a blender and blitz until very smooth. For a more refined finish, strain it through a fine sieve afterwards.

Whisk the egg whites until they form stiff peaks and gently fold in the grated cheese. Use 2 tablespoons to shape the mixture into quenelles: to do this, take a tablespoonful of the mixture and then shape it with the second spoon, turning it between the two. Or you can just scoop it into 8–12 balls. Bring the milk to a simmer in a large pan. Poach the quenelles in it for 3–4 minutes, until set, turning them over halfway through. Remove with a slotted spoon and drain well.

Add the cream to the soup and reheat without letting it boil, then season to taste. Pour into warm bowls and serve topped with the cheese meringues and some shavings of Emmenthal.

PG TIPS
You could poach the floating islands in water, but they have a better flavour if you use milk. Save the milk afterwards to make a cheese sauce, if you like.

Sometimes known as French Cheddar, Cantal is a very versatile cooking cheese and is particularly good in soups, sauces and gratins. It is at its best in late summer, when the milk is at its richest. Winter vegetables such as cabbage and carrots are often added to this soup along with the potatoes. I like to serve it with thin slices of toasted baguette rubbed with oil and garlic.

potato & **cantal** soup

SERVES 4

50g unsalted butter
600g potatoes, cut into slices
  1cm thick
250g leeks, white part only,
  finely sliced
3 garlic cloves, crushed
600ml Chicken or
  Vegetable Stock (see page 16)

90ml double cream
300ml milk, boiled & strained
175g mature Cantal
Salt & freshly ground black pepper

Alternative cheeses
Beaufort, Gruyère or Emmenthal

Heat the butter in a large saucepan, add the potatoes, leeks and garlic, then cover and sweat for 4–5 minutes. Pour in the stock and bring to the boil. Skim to remove any impurities from the surface, reduce the heat and simmer until the vegetables are just cooked. Add the cream and boiled milk and heat through gently, then stir in the grated Cantal. Remove from the heat, season to taste and serve.

This rustic Italian soup is very nourishing and quick and easy to make. All you do is pour a well-flavoured broth over slices of fried bread and then slip in an egg, which cooks in the heat of the broth. However, such simplicity relies on the finest ingredients for its success: don't make the soup unless you have homemade stock, good country-style bread and free-range eggs.

zuppa pavese

SERVES 4

6 fresh eggs
8 slices of white country-style bread,
  cut 1cm thick
100g Parmesan, grated
50g unsalted butter
1 litre Meat Stock (see page 17) or,
  better still, consommé
Salt & freshly ground black pepper

Beat 2 of the eggs in a bowl, season lightly, then pour them into a shallow dish. Dip the bread slices in the beaten egg on both sides, then dredge in 75g of the grated Parmesan. Heat the butter in a large frying pan and fry the bread until golden on both sides.

Put the slices of fried bread in 4 deep, heatproof serving bowls. Bring the stock or consommé to the boil and pour it over the bread to immerse it completely. Crack an egg into each bowl on top of the bread. Leave the bowls on the side of the stove or over a very low heat to allow the eggs to cook lightly. Serve with the remaining cheese on the side, for sprinkling over the soup.

PG TIPS
If you prefer, you can poach the eggs in the hot stock in a saucepan, then place them on the fried bread in the soup bowls and pour the soup over.

This soup dates back to my early days at Inigo Jones restaurant in London's Covent Garden. I enjoy preparing and tasting it as much now as I did then. You can make the soup without the oysters and it's still good, but they do give it an incomparable scent and flavour.

white cabbage & oyster broth with **fourme d'ambert** cheese

SERVES 4

50g unsalted butter
200g white cabbage, cut into
  2cm dice
1 teaspoon cumin seeds
1 litre Vegetable Stock or Chicken
  Stock (see page 16)
12 fresh oysters
50g Fourme d'Ambert
5 tablespoons double cream
1 tablespoon chopped fresh chives
  (optional)
Salt & freshly ground black pepper

Alternative cheeses
Dunsyre Blue, Cashel Blue or
Dovedale

Melt the butter in a saucepan, add the cabbage, then cover and sweat for 5–8 minutes. Stir in the cumin seeds, pour in the stock and bring to the boil. Skim off any impurities that rise to the surface and simmer gently for about 15 minutes, until the cabbage is tender.

Meanwhile, open the oyster shells and remove the oysters, reserving their juice (see Tip on page 30). Cut the oysters in half and strain the juice through a piece of muslin. Set aside.

Pass the Fourme d'Ambert cheese through a fine sieve and blend it with the cream. Stir the cream into the soup and adjust the seasoning. Add the cleaned oysters together with their strained juice, sprinkle with the chives, if using, and serve immediately.

PG TIPS
On no account let the soup boil after the cheese and cream mixture has been added to it or the delicate flavour will be spoiled. If the briny taste of oysters is not to your liking, you may prefer to substitute mussels. Simply cook the mussels with a little water until they open, then strain the cooking juices into the soup.

A heartwarming, lightly spiced soup topped with stringy fontina cheese and spiked with lemon. Serve with chunks of fresh bread.

cannellini bean soup with **fontina gremolata**

SERVES 4

50g unsalted butter
75g onions, diced
1 garlic clove, crushed
200g cannellini beans, soaked
 overnight & then drained
50g carrot, diced
1/2 red chilli, deseeded & finely
 chopped
2 ripe tomatoes, chopped
2 cardamom pods, crushed
1 teaspoon cumin seeds
1.3 litres Chicken Stock or
 Vegetable Stock (see page 16)
Salt & freshly ground black pepper

For the gremolata
75g fontina, very finely grated
1 tablespoon finely grated
 lemon zest
1 tablespoon fresh thyme leaves
2 garlic cloves, crushed

Alternative cheeses
Raclette, Taleggio, Port Salut or
Cornish Yarg

Melt the butter in a pan over a medium heat, add the onions and garlic and sauté for 4–5 minutes, until softened. Add the cannellini beans, carrot, chilli and tomatoes, then cover and cook gently for 5 minutes. Next, stir in the cardamom, cumin seeds and stock and bring to the boil. Reduce the heat and simmer for 1–1½ hours, or until the beans are tender. Pour the soup into a blender and blitz to a purée, then strain it through a fine sieve to give a creamy texture. Adjust the seasoning and reheat gently.

For the gremolata, mix all the ingredients together in a bowl. Pour the soup into warm bowls, scatter with the gremolata and serve straight away.

PG TIPS
Other pulses such as lentils can be used with just as good effect. I sometimes leave the beans whole and top them with the gremolata to serve as a winter stew.

The surprising thing about this recipe is the stunning contrast of hot and cold. The chilled smooth gazpacho is poured around stuffed tomatoes that have come straight from the oven. The soup is strongly scented with basil, which I love to use in large quantities, but you can always reduce the amount if you prefer or if you don't have much available.

tomato gazpacho with **cabécou**-stuffed tomatoes

SERVES 4

900g overripe plum tomatoes
  (or use half plum tomatoes, half
  beef tomatoes)
1 tablespoon tomato ketchup
1 tablespoon olive oil
1 small garlic clove, peeled
1 tablespoon caster sugar
150ml Vegetable Stock (see page 16)
A bunch of fresh basil
2 tablespoons red wine vinegar
2 tablespoons dry vermouth
Salt & freshly ground white pepper

For the stuffed tomatoes
2 Cabécou cheeses or other small,
  firm goat's cheeses
1/2 onion, very finely chopped
1 small courgette, very finely
  chopped
1 egg yolk
25g mixed fresh herbs, such as
  basil, chervil, parsley & chives,
  finely chopped
2–3 tablespoons fresh white
  breadcrumbs
8 ripe but firm small tomatoes
A little olive oil for brushing

For the soup, blanch the tomatoes in boiling water for 1 minute, then drain and refresh in ice-cold water. Drain again and peel. Cut the tomatoes in half and put them in a bowl with the tomato ketchup, olive oil, garlic, sugar, vegetable stock and leaves from the bunch of basil, reserving 8–12 leaves for garnishing the finished dish. Stir in the red wine vinegar and vermouth, season lightly and leave to marinate for 1–2 hours.

Strain the tomato mixture through a fine sieve into a bowl, pushing hard to extract all the juice (don't use a blender or the fresh colour of the tomatoes will be lost). Adjust the seasoning, then chill until ready to serve.

For the stuffed tomatoes, preheat the oven to 180°C, 350°F, gas 4. Put the goat's cheese in a bowl and crush with a fork. Stir in the onion, courgette, egg yolk and herbs, then add enough breadcrumbs to bind the mixture lightly together. Season to taste. Slice a lid off the top of each tomato and reserve. Carefully scoop out the pulp and seeds from the tomatoes with a spoon. Fill them with the stuffing, brush with a little olive oil and bake for 5 minutes, until soft and heated through.

Place 2 stuffed tomatoes in each soup plate and replace their lids, then carefully pour the gazpacho around. Decorate with the reserved basil leaves and serve immediately.

PG TIPS
Make this soup in late summer when overripe tomatoes are being sold off cheaply. I strongly recommend that you keep this delicate, fresh-tasting soup for the summer months, as tomatoes have less flavour, juice and sweetness in winter.

According to a recent survey, by far the most popular vegetable dish in the UK is cauliflower cheese. Let's face it, it's something we all enjoy. So why not try cauliflower cheese soup?

cauliflower **cheese** soup

SERVES 4

1 large cauliflower, weighing
 about 750g
50g unsalted butter
1 onion, thinly sliced
1 leek, thinly sliced
1 litre Vegetable Stock (see page 16)
 or water
2 egg yolks
4 tablespoons double cream
75g farmhouse Cheddar, grated
Freshly grated nutmeg
Salt & freshly ground black pepper

Alternative cheeses
A soft goat's cheese or Yorkshire
Blue, Buxton Blue or Gorwydd
Caerphilly

Trim the outer green leaves off the cauliflower and cut it into florets. Heat the butter in a heavy-based saucepan, add the onion and leek, then cover and cook gently for 2–3 minutes, until the vegetables begin to soften. Do not let them brown. Add the cauliflower florets (reserving a few small ones as a garnish) and cook gently for 4–5 minutes. Pour in the stock or water, bring to the boil, then reduce the heat and simmer for 20–25 minutes, until the cauliflower is very tender. Meanwhile, cook the reserved cauliflower florets in boiling salted water until just tender. Drain, refresh in cold water, then drain again well and reserve.

Purée the soup in a blender until smooth, return it to the saucepan and bring to the boil. In a bowl, lightly whisk together the egg yolks, cream and cheese. Whisk about 6 tablespoons of the soup into this mixture, then stir it back into the remainder of the soup; do not let it boil. Season with nutmeg, salt and pepper, then serve garnished with the cooked cauliflower florets.

Here a rustic soup made from the humble potato is transformed into something magical with the addition of creamy rosary goat's cheese, lifted with a little truffle oil.

potato & **rosary** soup with truffle oil

SERVES 4

50g unsalted butter
1 onion, chopped
200g leeks, sliced
200g new potatoes, peeled and diced
900ml chicken stock
100ml double cream
75g rosary goat's cheese
1 tablespoon white truffle oil
Salt & freshly ground black pepper

Heat the butter in a large pan, add the onion and leeks and cook over a low heat for 8–10 minutes without colouring. Add the potatoes and cook for a further 3 minutes. Add the prepared stock and bring to the boil. Then reduce the heat and cook for 15 minutes or until tender.

In a separate pan heat the cream to the boil, then stir in the cheese and allow it to melt.

Place the potato soup in a blender and blitz to a purée. Mix in the goat's cheese cream and the truffle oil. Season to taste and serve immediately.

PG TIPS
As an alternative to potato, Jerusalem artichoke and cauliflower are equally successful. The soup should be the consistency of single cream. If it is too thick, simply thin down with more chicken stock.

Lincolnshire Poacher is a full flavoured, unpasteurised milk cheese with a similar taste to a classic Cheddar, but with a more open texture. With its pale yellow hue and incredible brown rind, it has won numerous awards.

lobster & **lincolnshire poacher** bisque

SERVES 4

1 cooked lobster, weighing
  about 750g
75g unsalted butter
1/2 onion, roughly chopped
1 celery stick, roughly chopped
1 carrot, roughly chopped
2 garlic cloves, crushed
2 tablespoons tomato purée
4 tablespoons cognac
150ml dry white wine
1 tablespoon fresh tarragon leaves,
  plus a few sprigs to garnish
75g plain flour
1 litre Chicken Stock (see page 16)
150ml double cream
75g Lincolnshire Poacher, grated
Cayenne pepper
Salt & freshly ground black pepper

Split the lobster in half down the back: the easiest way to do this is to put a large knife through the centre of the body section and cut down through the head, then take out the knife, turn the lobster round and cut down the centre of the body through the tail. Remove and discard the head sac and the intestinal vein, then remove the cooked lobster flesh from the head and tail. Crack the claws in 2 or 3 places and pick out the meat. Place the lobster shells in a bowl and, using a meat hammer, crush them into smallish pieces. This helps to extract maximum flavour.

Heat the butter in a heavy-based pan, add the crushed lobster shells and fry for 4–5 minutes, until they begin to turn golden. Add the vegetables and garlic and fry for 5 minutes, until softened. Stir in the tomato purée, then add the cognac, white wine and tarragon leaves and cook for 5 minutes. Stir in the flour and cook for a further 5 minutes. Add the stock, bring to the boil and skim off any impurities that rise to the surface. Reduce the heat and simmer for 30–40 minutes.

Meanwhile, dice the lobster flesh and set aside. Bring the cream to the boil in a separate pan, then remove from the heat. Add the cheese and stir until melted and smooth, then set aside.

Blitz the soup in a blender until the shells are quite finely ground, then pass it through a very fine sieve and stir in the cheese cream. Add cayenne, salt and pepper to taste, then pour the soup into warm bowls. Garnish with the diced lobster and sprigs of tarragon, dust very lightly with cayenne and serve.

PG TIPS
Rice may be used instead of flour to thicken the soup. It is important that you do not cook the stock for longer than 40 minutes, as it will lose its natural flavours and become bitter. If you decide to use crab instead of lobster, cook the live crabs for 12–15 minutes, depending on their size.

Like Zuppa Pavese (see page 54), this is an Italian peasant-style soup. I love the simplicity of it, made with just a few basic ingredients and a little care. It makes thrifty use of leftovers but you must have good-quality stock and good-quality olive oil. And you should not neglect the lemon; however strange it may sound, it really does give a little lift to this heart-warming one-pot soup.

bread & **pecorino** soup

SERVES 4

1 litre Chicken Stock (see page 16)
4 tablespoons olive oil
2 garlic cloves, crushed
275g potatoes, peeled & cut into small cubes
4 thick slices of stale Italian country bread, cut into cubes

6 tablespoons grated pecorino
1 tablespoon coarsely chopped fresh marjoram
1/4 teaspoon grated lemon zest
Salt
Cracked black pepper (see Tip on page 146)

Bring the stock to the boil with 3 tablespoons of the olive oil, add the garlic and potatoes and return to the boil. Add the bread cubes and simmer for 20–25 minutes, until the potatoes are tender. Remove the pan from the heat and stir in the pecorino, marjoram and lemon zest. Season with a little salt and a sprinkling of freshly cracked black pepper. Drizzle over the remaining olive oil and serve straight away.

This variation on the classic French onion soup replaces the usual white wine and Gruyère with ingredients from Normandy – beer and Camembert cheese. I have successfully replaced the Camembert with Carré de l'Est, which is milder in flavour and has a delicate aroma when ripe. You can, of course, use grated Gruyère or Emmenthal for a more traditional onion soup.

french onion soup with beer & **camembert**

SERVES 4

75g unsalted butter
300g onions, sliced
1/2 tablespoon sugar
1 tablespoon plain flour
1 teaspoon tomato purée
100ml light beer
1 litre Meat Stock (see page 17)

1 ficelle (small, thin baguette) or 2 crusty bread rolls, thinly sliced & toasted
100g Camembert, rind removed, thinly sliced
Salt & freshly ground black pepper

Alternative cheeses
Carré de l'Est, Gruyère, Emmenthal

Heat the butter in a heavy-based pan, add the onions and sugar and cook over a medium heat for at least 20 minutes, until very soft, golden and caramelised. Stir in the flour and tomato purée and cook for 2 minutes, until they brown very slightly. Pour in the beer, bring to the boil and after 1 minute add the stock. Reduce the heat and simmer for 15–20 minutes, then season to taste. Pour the soup into 4 heatproof soup bowls or 1 large tureen and float the toasted bread on top in a single layer. Cover this with the Camembert slices. Put the bowls under a hot grill (or in a hot oven) until the cheese forms a well-browned crust. Serve immediately.

A beautifully delicate vegetable chowder spiked with aromatic saffron and coriander. Saffron is now much more readily available, and imports from Spain and the Middle East continue to improve. It is an expensive spice but it has no substitute, especially in this chowder. Sachets of powdered saffron are cheaper than saffron strands but they cannot compete with them in flavour – always buy the real thing.

saffron vegetable chowder with coriander & **goat's cheese** pesto

SERVES 4

3 tablespoons olive oil
1 garlic clove, crushed
1 leek, 1 carrot, 1 celery stick,
  1 courgette, 1 potato, all cut into
  5mm dice
1 litre Vegetable Stock
  or Chicken Stock (see page 16)
A pinch of saffron strands
2 tomatoes, skinned, deseeded & cut
  into 5mm dice
2 tablespoons Coriander & Goat's
  Cheese Pesto (see page 20)
125ml milk
Salt & freshly ground black pepper

Heat the olive oil in a heavy-based pan, together with the garlic. Next, add the leek, carrot, celery, courgette and potato and cook for 2 minutes over a low heat.

Add the stock and saffron and bring to the boil. Reduce the heat and simmer for 20–25 minutes, until the vegetables are tender. Add the tomatoes and pesto and stir thoroughly, then add the milk. Season to taste with salt and pepper and serve immediately.

PG TIPS
As an effective variation, replace the coriander and goat's cheese pesto with fresh herbs, such as parsley, basil or chives.

chapter 3 **salads**

The simplest of tomato salads, topped with a creamy dressing made with goat's cheese and goat's milk. Serve as an accompaniment or as part of a selection of salads for a picnic.

plum tomato salad with **goat's milk** dressing

SERVES 4

8 large, ripe but firm plum tomatoes,
  cut into slices 5mm thick
75g Roubiliac or Golden Cross
  goat's cheese
90ml goat's milk
2 tablespoons Greek yogurt
1 tablespoon chopped fresh basil
1 tablespoon chopped fresh oregano
1/2 tablespoon chopped fresh
  coriander
Salt & freshly ground black pepper

Arrange the tomato slices in overlapping circles in a shallow serving bowl. Season with salt and pepper. Whisk all the remaining ingredients together and pour over the tomatoes. Serve well chilled.

PG TIPS

If you can't find goat's milk, cow's milk works well, too. I personally see no gain in removing the tomato skins for this salad, especially in summer when tomatoes are at their best. It is, of course, a matter of choice, and others may like to blanch them briefly in boiling water before peeling off the skins. Chives, parsley or chervil would make excellent alternative herbs, but they must be fresh.

I love the smoky flavours that predominate in this salad. The tart vinaigrette makes an ideal dressing for the charred leeks. If possible, cook the vegetables on a barbecue.

blackened leek, red onion & smoked **mozzarella** salad with tarragon vinaigrette

SERVES 4

A pinch of sugar
24 young leeks, trimmed
2 red onions, cut into wedges
1 smoked mozzarella cheese, cut
  into 8 thin slices
Salt & freshly ground black pepper

For the vinaigrette
3 tablespoons tarragon vinegar
  or champagne vinegar
1 teaspoon Dijon mustard
1 tablespoon chopped fresh tarragon
135ml extra-virgin olive oil
1 tomato, deseeded & finely diced
1 tablespoon superfine capers,
  rinsed & drained
1 tablespoon green olives, stoned &
  finely chopped
1 hard-boiled egg, chopped

Alternative cheeses
Buffalo mozzarella or a goat's
cheese, such as coarsely
grated crottin

Bring a large pan of water to the boil with the sugar and a little salt. Throw in the leeks, return to the boil and cook gently for 2–3 minutes. Drain them well and dry on a cloth.

For the vinaigrette, mix the vinegar, mustard and tarragon together in a bowl and then whisk in the olive oil. Add all the remaining ingredients and season to taste with salt and pepper.

Grill the leeks and onions – for the best flavour this should be done on a barbecue or a ridged cast-iron grill pan, but you can also cook them under a preheated grill. When they are tender and slightly blackened, remove from the heat and season with salt and pepper.

Toss the leeks and onions with the vinaigrette and adjust the seasoning. Arrange on 4 serving plates, drape 2 slices of mozzarella over each portion and serve.

PG TIPS
Smoked mozzarella may not be a recognised household cheese, yet for me it is one of the nicest smoked cheeses. It is worth seeking out but, if you have a problem finding it, a creamy-tasting natural mozzarella would be fine.

The dark greeny-blue French lentilles du Puy are generally considered to have the best flavour and are well worth buying. They have recently been granted appellation d'origine contrôlée status, just like a fine wine or cheese, which means that only lentils from a particular corner of France – the area around Puy-en-Velay in the Haute Loire – are entitled to be called Puy. This decree is causing consternation among some British supermarket chains, which sell 'Puy lentils' that have in fact been produced in Canada. If you can't get the genuine article, don't worry! Cannellini beans also work very well in this winter salad.

warm lentil salad with pepper-grilled **goat's cheese** & anchovy toasts

SERVES 4

200g Puy lentils
1 onion, finely chopped
1 teaspoon cumin seeds
4 tablespoons olive oil
2 tablespoons balsamic vinegar or
  white wine vinegar
1 shallot, finely chopped

For the toasts
6 canned anchovy fillets, rinsed
  & dried
1 egg yolk
5 tablespoons olive oil
4 slices of French bread,
  cut 1.5cm thick
4 Capricorn goat's cheeses, cut
  horizontally in half
1 tablespoon fresh thyme or
  rosemary leaves
1 tablespoon coarsely ground
  black peppercorns

Alternative cheese
4 crottins, cut horizontally in half
or Tasmania Highland Chevre
(AUS)

Put the lentils in a saucepan, cover with cold water and bring to the boil, skimming off any impurities that rise to the surface. Add the onion and cumin seeds and simmer for 30–40 minutes, until the lentils are just tender. Drain them well. Mix the olive oil, vinegar and shallot together and stir into the lentils. Keep warm.

For the cheese and anchovy toasts, work the anchovies and egg yolk to a paste with a pestle and mortar, then gradually blend in the olive oil to give a thick purée. Toast the French bread and spread with the anchovy paste, then top each one with 2 pieces of goat's cheese. Sprinkle over the thyme or rosemary leaves and black pepper and place under a hot grill until lightly browned. Put the warm lentils on serving plates, top with the toasts and serve straight away.

PG TIPS
Because the quantities for the anchovy paste are small, you really need to use a pestle and mortar. However, if you double the amount, you can blitz everything together in a blender. You are bound to find a use for the surplus; store it in the refrigerator and toss with pasta or use in sandwiches.

For me, the combination of spinach and blue cheese is a spectacular one. Any type of blue cheese is suitable for this wonderfully fresh-tasting salad, scattered with nutritious pumpkin seeds. Just use your favourite.

spinach, **blue cheese** & avocado salad with pumpkin seeds

SERVES 4

350g tender young spinach leaves
100g mushrooms, sliced
2 hard-boiled eggs, chopped
75g blue cheese, in 1cm cubes
1 garlic clove, crushed
200g fromage frais
1 teaspoon mild Dijon mustard
1 teaspoon lemon juice
1 avocado, peeled, stoned & cut into
  1cm cubes
12 slices of small baguette, toasted
50g pumpkin seeds, toasted
Salt & freshly ground black pepper

Put the spinach in a salad bowl and add the mushrooms, hard-boiled eggs and blue cheese. Mix together the garlic, fromage frais, mustard and lemon juice to make a dressing and toss carefully with the salad. Season to taste.

Arrange on serving plates, top with the avocado and toasted baguette slices and sprinkle over the toasted pumpkin seeds. Serve immediately.

PG TIPS
Other vegetables, such as leeks, artichokes and even asparagus, can be prepared in the same way for this salad. Pumpkin seeds are quite easy to find in health shops, but sunflower seeds make a tasty alternative if necessary.

Jarlsberg cheese is said by many to be a copy of the famous Swiss Emmenthal. I personally think it has a more delicate flavour and not such a nutty aftertaste. It is one of Norway's proudest treasures and deserves to be better known and more frequently used.

salad of pickled herrings, **jarlsberg**, potatoes & dill

SERVES 4

500g pickled herrings
400g waxy potatoes
1 red onion, finely chopped
2 tablespoons white wine vinegar
6 tablespoons olive oil
1 tablespoon crème fraîche

2 tablespoons chopped fresh dill
1 tablespoon sweet mustard
150g Jarlsberg
Salt & freshly ground black pepper

Alternative cheeses
Emmenthal, Cheddar, Havarti
or Tilsit

Cut the pickled herrings into large chunks and the Jarlsberg into batons. Cook the potatoes in boiling salted water until just tender, then drain. Leave until cool enough to handle, then peel and cut in half. Put them in a bowl and add the herrings and red onion. Mix together the vinegar, oil, crème fraîche, dill and mustard to make a dressing. Pour the dressing over the potatoes, herrings and onions and toss lightly together, then season to taste. Transfer to a serving bowl, top with the batons of Jarlsberg and serve.

I am very fond of this salad. It always finds a place on my winter menus and is extremely pretty. The crunch of red cabbage and roasted walnuts makes an excellent combination with the sharp and tangy Roquefort. If Roquefort is not available, any blue cheese could be substituted, but I find the stronger ones such as Gorgonzola work best.

roquefort & red cabbage salad with roasted walnut vinaigrette

SERVES 4

¼ red cabbage, central core
  removed, thinly sliced
4 tablespoons red wine vinegar
50g caster sugar
600ml water
100g streaky bacon, cut into 2cm dice
2 slices of white bread, cut into
  1cm cubes
1 garlic clove, crushed
2 heads of chicory
1 small head of radicchio
150g Roquefort, crumbled
Salt & freshly ground black pepper

For the vinaigrette
4 tablespoons red wine vinegar
1 teaspoon Dijon mustard
4 tablespoons walnut oil
4 tablespoons olive oil
2 tablespoons walnuts, roasted (see
  Tip) & broken into chunks

Alternative cheeses
Any blue cheese, especially Valdeon

Put the cabbage in a bowl. Bring the vinegar to the boil, add the sugar and, once dissolved, pour it over the cabbage and stir well. Boil the water and pour that over the cabbage too. Leave to soak for 5 minutes, then drain in a colander and leave to cool.

Heat a frying pan over a high heat, add the bacon and cook until it is crisp and the fat has been released. Add the bread and fry until golden, then stir in the garlic and fry for 1 minute. Remove from the heat. Put the red cabbage in a salad bowl with the chicory and radicchio leaves, scatter over the bacon and croûtons and the Roquefort cheese.

Whisk together all the ingredients for the vinaigrette and pour it over the salad. Toss well, adjust the seasoning and serve.

PG TIPS
To roast nuts, toss them in a little oil, season lightly, then place on a baking sheet and bake in an oven preheated to 180°C, 350°F, gas 4 for 5–8 minutes, or until toasted in flavour and colour. Cool before use. I have on occasion replaced the red cabbage with finely shredded beetroot: a great alternative summer salad.

Many years ago I worked in the West Country and discovered just how good the local ingredients could be. If you can get Cornish crab to use in this dish, for example, you will find it has an incomparable flavour. The salad makes a good first course for an early-summer meal.

cornish crab & asparagus salad with lemon, mustard & **parmesan** vinaigrette

SERVES 4

12 asparagus spears, peeled & well trimmed
2 heads of chicory
2 avocados, peeled, stoned & sliced
2 carrots, cut into matchsticks
300g fresh white crabmeat
Parmesan shavings, to garnish
Salt & freshly ground black pepper

For the lemon, mustard & Parmesan vinaigrette
1 tablespoon Dijon mustard
1 small egg yolk
1 tablespoon lemon juice
Finely grated zest of 1/4 lemon
1 tablespoon champagne vinegar or white wine vinegar
5 tablespoons extra-virgin olive oil
1 1/2 tablespoons freshly grated Parmesan

Cook the asparagus spears in boiling salted water for 3–4 minutes or until just tender. Drain and refresh in cold water, then dry them thoroughly and cut lengthways in half.

For the dressing, whisk together the mustard, egg yolk, lemon juice and zest and vinegar, then whisk in the olive oil. Add the grated Parmesan cheese and season to taste.

Pull the leaves from the chicory, wash and dry them and arrange in a salad bowl or on serving plates. Put the asparagus, avocado, carrots and crabmeat in a separate bowl and toss gently with the dressing, then adjust the seasoning. Scatter this mixture over the chicory leaves, sprinkle some coarsely cracked black pepper over the top (see Tip on page 146) and then scatter with the Parmesan shavings. Serve immediately.

PG TIPS
Vegetarians can easily omit the crabmeat and replace it with more vegetables. Globe artichoke hearts, for example, would go rather well.

In this tangy salad the oranges are marinated in vinegar and sugar overnight to give a refreshing sweet-and-sour flavour. Feta is a much-copied cheese and consequently the quality and flavour vary greatly, as does the type of milk used. Always try to obtain genuine Greek feta, which is generally made of 30 per cent goat's milk and 70 per cent sheep's milk.

chilli-pickled orange, **feta** & olive salad

SERVES 4

4 oranges, preferably navel
90ml white wine vinegar
3 tablespoons caster sugar
1 red chilli, thinly sliced into rings
90ml olive oil
2 tablespoons black olives, stoned
175g feta, cut into 1cm cubes
1 tablespoon chopped fresh oregano
  or parsley
Baby spinach and rocket leaves, to
  garnish (optional)
Salt & freshly ground black pepper

Alternative cheeses
Haloumi or a firm goat's cheese

Peel the oranges, being sure to remove all the white pith, and cut them into slices 5mm thick. Remove any pips and put the orange slices in a shallow dish. Boil the vinegar and sugar together for 2–3 minutes, add the chilli and then pour on to the orange slices. Cover and leave overnight.

The next day, drain off the juices from the pickled oranges into a bowl. Whisk in the olive oil to make a dressing and season with salt and pepper. Arrange the oranges in a serving bowl. Stir the olives, feta and oregano or parsley into the dressing and sprinkle it over the oranges. Sprinkle with coarsely cracked black pepper (see Tip on page 146), scatter over the spinach and rocket leaves, if using, and serve.

PG TIPS
Some people like to soak feta cheese in warm water or milk before using. This effectively softens the strong, salty flavour.

Radicchio is a bitter salad leaf that to my mind needs a contrasting partner. The blue cheese yogurt dressing fits the bill perfectly. You could add some chopped hard-boiled egg, potatoes and French beans to make a more substantial dish for a main course.

radicchio, mushroom & chive salad with **blue cheese** yogurt dressing

SERVES 4

2 heads of radicchio
300g button mushrooms, sliced
1 bunch of fresh chives
Salt & freshly ground black pepper

For the blue cheese yogurt dressing
50g Stilton
1 tablespoon champagne vinegar
5 tablespoons crème fraîche
3 tablespoons Greek yogurt
Juice of 1/2 lemon
Freshly grated nutmeg
1 tablespoon chopped fresh chives

Alternative cheeses
Roquefort, dolcelatte or Cambazola

First make the dressing. Put the Stilton in a bowl and mash well with a fork. Stir in the vinegar, then gently whisk in the crème fraîche and yogurt. Squeeze in the lemon juice and season to taste with nutmeg, salt and pepper, then fold in the chives.

Separate the radicchio leaves, wash them and dry them well. Place in a bowl, add the sliced mushrooms and season lightly. Add the blue cheese dressing and toss carefully, then adjust the seasoning to taste. Arrange on serving plates, snip the chives into pieces 1cm long and scatter over the top. Serve immediately.

PG TIPS
If you prefer a less tart dressing, add 1 tablespoon warmed honey, maple syrup or even good old sugar. Try adding a little grated orange rind to the dressing, too. Belgian endive or chicory has a similar bitter taste and could easily be substituted for the radicchio.

This hearty salad of cheese, ham and potatoes is substantial enough to serve as a main course. Salads that combine cheese and meat are very common in northern Europe. I devised this one with Italian flavourings in mind. The recipe has been in my repertoire since my early days as a chef and has remained one of my favourite salads. The original salad consists of shavings of Tête de Moine (monk's head), a cheese native to Switzerland. It is rather expensive and a little difficult to find except in specialist cheese shops, but well worth enquiring about. Fontina makes a more accessible and good substitute.

insalata di **fontina**

SERVES 4

225g new potatoes
50g prosciutto, cut into strips
100g fontina, cut into batons
50g mortadella, cut into batons
6 cocktail gherkins, cut lengthways
 into quarters
1 red onion, sliced into thin rings
Salt & freshly ground black pepper

For the dressing
1 tablespoon chopped fresh oregano
1/4 teaspoon Dijon mustard
2 canned anchovy fillets
2 tablespoons white wine vinegar
6 tablespoons olive oil

Alternative cheeses
Gruyère, Emmenthal, Port Salut,
Jarlsberg or Leerdammer

For the dressing, place the oregano and the mustard in a small bowl. Rinse the anchovy fillets to extract their salty flavour, then drain. Dry them well and chop finely. Add them to the bowl, pour over the vinegar and mix well together. Add the olive oil and whisk to form a light dressing. Season to taste and set aside.

Cook the potatoes in boiling salted water for about 20 minutes until just tender, then remove and cool slightly before peeling. Cut into 5mm thick slices and place in a bowl. While the potatoes are still warm, pour over the dressing and leave for 20 minutes to allow them to soak up the flavours.

Add the remaining ingredients and mix together. Pour on the dressing and toss again. Adjust the seasoning and serve.

Lamb and mint form a combination that everyone knows. I took it a stage further to create this wonderful salad. We are fortunate that we can still buy the Scottish cheese Lanark Blue. In 1995 its producer, Humphrey Errington, fought a 13-month battle in the courts to defend its reputation against health officials, who claimed that as a raw-milk cheese it could contain the bacterium Listeria and thus cause food poisoning. He finally won his case, and small cheesemakers throughout the UK owe him a huge debt for demonstrating that cheese made from unpasteurized milk carries no more risk to health than pasteurized cheese.

salad of grilled lamb fillet with **lanark blue** & warm mint dressing

SERVES 4

4 lamb fillets, about 75g each
100g French beans
8–12 thin slices cut from a ficelle
  loaf or small baguette
Olive oil, for brushing
A handful each of frisée & spinach
  leaves
2 tomatoes, skinned, deseeded &
  cut into strips
65g button mushrooms, thinly sliced
50g Lanark Blue, diced
Salt & freshly ground black pepper

For the dressing
4 tablespoons double cream
1 tablespoon clear honey
50g Lanark Blue, crumbled
1 tablespoon sherry vinegar
2 tablespoons olive oil
1 tablespoon chopped fresh mint
2 tablespoons hot water

Alternative cheeses
Stilton, Danish Blue, Bleu
d'Auvergne, Buxton Blue or King
Island (AUS)

Season the lamb fillets and cook on a ridged cast-iron grill pan (or under a hot grill or in a frying pan) for 5–8 minutes, until done but still rosy inside. Keep warm.

Meanwhile, cook the French beans in boiling salted water until just tender, then drain and refresh in cold water. Drain again and dry.

For the dressing, put the cream and honey in a pan and bring to the boil, then remove from the heat. Add the cheese and allow it to melt into the cream. Whisk in the vinegar, olive oil and mint, then whisk in the water and season to taste.

Brush the slices of bread with olive oil and grill on both sides until they are lightly browned.

Put the frisée and spinach leaves in a bowl, add the tomatoes, French beans, mushrooms and cheese, then toss with the warm dressing. Put in the centre of 4 serving plates. Slice the grilled lamb fillets and arrange around the salad. Top the salad with the croûtons and serve immediately.

chapter 4 **pasta, pizza, rice & gnocchi**

A great and simple dish. When all that is needed is something quick but tasty, this fits the bill perfectly. Try adding crisply fried, diced pancetta to the pasta.

tagliatelle with fried egg, capers & **pecorino** sardo

SERVES 4

500g tagliatelle
Freshly grated nutmeg
40g unsalted butter
2 tablespoons superfine capers,
  rinsed & drained
4 free-range eggs
A little clarified butter (see Tip)
100g pecorino Sardo, cut
  into shavings
Salt & freshly ground black pepper

Cook the pasta in boiling salted water until al dente, then drain well and return to the pan. Season with nutmeg, salt and pepper, add the butter and capers and toss together well. Keep warm.

Quickly fry the eggs in clarified butter and season with salt. Arrange the pasta on warmed serving plates, top each portion with a fried egg and scatter over the pecorino shavings. Sprinkle with a little freshly cracked black pepper (see Tip on page 146) and serve.

PG TIPS
To clarify butter, heat gently in a small pan until it begins to boil. Boil for 2 minutes, then pour off the clarified butter through a fine conical strainer or a muslin-lined sieve, leaving the white, milky sediment in the pan. You should store clarified butter in the refrigerator.

Make this dish during the autumnal months of the year, when a vast array of exciting mushrooms become available. If you are lucky enough to use wild mushrooms use 300g of your favourite variety but, as these are not always within everyone's grasp, I have used the more commonly available dried mushrooms.

funghi **carbonara**

SERVES 4

450g fresh/dried spaghetti or linguini
100g diced pancetta
25g unsalted butter
20g dried mixed wild mushrooms
  (soaked in hot water for 1 hour)
1 shallot, finely chopped
150ml double cream
2 eggs beaten
100g grated parmesan
Salt, freshly ground pepper &
  ground nutmeg

Alternative cheese
Pecorino

Cook the pasta in a large pan of boiling salted water, until al dente then drain well in a colander.

Fry the pancetta until crispy. Heat the butter in a large frying pan, drain the mushrooms from their water and add to the pan. Add the shallots and cook together for 3–4 minutes until softened. Add the pancetta.

Pour over the cream and cook for 2–3 minutes until the sauce has thickened slightly.

Add the drained pasta and stir in the beaten eggs and cheese. Toss well together and season with salt, pepper and nutmeg. Serve immediately.

Although I have used bucatini pasta for this recipe, other pastas such as linguini and fettucine are equally suitable. Whenever I make this simple dish at home it transports me to the Greek Islands in an instant. Hot pickled chillies are available from Middle Eastern delicatessens.

bucatini with **feta**, pickled chilli, tomato & mint

SERVES 4

4 tablespoons good quality olive oil
1 small garlic clove. crushed
450g bucatini
3 tablespoons chopped fresh mint
4 ripe but firm plum tomatoes
  cut into $\frac{1}{2}$cm dice
300g Greek feta, cut into small
  $\frac{1}{2}$cm dice
2 small hot pickled chillies,
  finely chopped

Alternative cheeses
Mozzarella

Heat half the oil in a large frying pan over a medium heat, add the garlic and cook for 1 minute until it becomes translucent. Stir in the mint, add the chopped tomatoes and diced feta and cook for a further 2–3 minutes.

Meanwhile, cook the bucatini in a large pan of boiling salted water until al dente. Drain the pasta in a colander and add to the pan. Add the pickled chillies and toss the mixture together.

Divide the pasta between 4 serving pasta bowls and drizzle over the remaining oil.

PG TIPS
The addition of a few chopped black olives to this dish is very pleasing.

Crumbly cottage or curd cheese is used extensively in many German dishes. I particularly like the stuffing for this ravioli.

topfenravioli with prosciutto, spinach & foaming brown butter

SERVES 4

75g unsalted butter
450g young spinach leaves
100g cottage cheese, well drained
75g prosciutto, finely diced
50g buffalo or cow's milk
  mozzarella, finely diced
2 tablespoons freshly grated
  Parmesan, plus extra to serve
10 fresh basil leaves, roughly
  chopped, plus a few whole leaves
  to garnish
Freshly grated nutmeg
Salt & freshly ground black pepper

For the pasta dough
250g strong plain flour
A pinch of salt
1 tablespoon extra-virgin olive oil
2 eggs plus 1 egg yolk, lightly beaten

First make the pasta dough. Put the flour, salt and olive oil into a food processor and process for a few seconds to combine. Add the beaten eggs and process until the mixture forms a mass. This should only take a few seconds and it is important not to overwork the dough. Remove the dough from the food processor. It should be fairly soft and pliable. If it is too dry, knead in a little water; if it is too wet, sprinkle with a little flour. Cover with cling film and leave to rest at room temperature for 15–30 minutes.

Meanwhile, make the filling. Heat 25g of the butter in a large pan, add the spinach and cook for just a few minutes until it has wilted and all the excess moisture has evaporated. Transfer to a bowl and leave to cool, then chop finely. Stir in the cottage cheese, prosciutto, mozzarella, Parmesan and chopped basil. Season to taste with nutmeg, salt and pepper.

Roll out the dough using a pasta machine if you have one. Alternatively, divide it into 2 batches and roll it out very thinly by hand. It should be so thin that it is almost translucent. Lightly brush 1 sheet of the dough with water, then put teaspoonfuls of stuffing on it about 5cm apart, in rows. Cover with the second sheet of pasta, press down gently, then cut round the stuffing with a round 6cm fluted pastry cutter. Check that the edges of the ravioli are well sealed.

Cook the ravioli in plenty of gently simmering salted water for 2–3 minutes, until al dente, then drain well. Heat the remaining butter in a frying pan until it is foaming, golden brown and smells nutty (the bottom of the pan will be covered with brown butter specks). Immediately drizzle the butter over the ravioli and sprinkle with more freshly grated Parmesan and a few basil leaves before serving.

For an all-green version of this colourful pasta dish, you could substitute courgettes, leeks and broccoli for the peppers.

rigatoni with mixed peppers & coriander
& **goat's cheese** pesto

SERVES 4

4 peppers (1 red, 1 green, 1 yellow,
  1 orange)
50g unsalted butter
2 tablespoons olive oil
A pinch of sugar
450g rigatoni
1 quantity of Coriander & Goat's
  Cheese Pesto (see page 20)
Salt & freshly ground black pepper
Fresh coriander leaves, to garnish
  (optional)

Halve and deseed the peppers, then cut them into strips 5mm wide. Heat the butter and oil in a frying pan, add the pepper strips and cook gently for 10–15 minutes. If they begin to stick to the pan, add a little water. When the peppers are tender, stir in the sugar and some salt and pepper to taste.

Cook the rigatoni in a large pan of boiling salted water until al dente, then drain well. Stir the pasta into the peppers, add the pesto sauce and lightly toss together. Adjust the seasoning, garnish with coriander leaves if liked, and serve straight away.

PG TIPS
For a really quick sauce, use bottled peppers in oil, and for a little variation why not try adding a few sautéed bacon lardons to the cooked pasta? Any other shaped pasta would look pretty in this dish.

Although I have used pennette for this dish, any type of pasta may be substituted. To offset the richness of the sauce, I sometimes top the pasta with a light herb salad of basil, chives and oregano, mixed with a little frisée and dressed with balsamic vinaigrette.

pennette al **dolcelatte**

SERVES 4

450g pennette
90ml double cream
100ml Chicken Stock or Vegetable
  Stock (see page 16)
90g dolcelatte, crumbled
4 tablespoons extra-virgin olive oil
Freshly grated nutmeg
Salt & freshly ground black pepper
Freshly grated Parmesan, to serve
  (optional)

Alternative cheese
Try dolcelatte torta, which is a combination of mascarpone and dolcelatte, and omit the double cream

Cook the pennette in plenty of boiling salted water until al dente. Meanwhile, bring the cream and stock to the boil, then remove from the heat and stir in the dolcelatte until smooth. Whisk in the olive oil to form a light sauce.

Drain the pasta and return it to the saucepan. Season with nutmeg, salt and pepper, then toss the pasta with the sauce. Serve immediately, with grated Parmesan if liked.

Calzone means pair of trousers! It is a sort of folded pizza, rather like a pasty, and is particularly delicious if you include lots of cheese so the molten cheese spills out when you cut into it. You can vary the fillings to your own taste – try mozzarella, salami or vegetables.

bel paese calzoni

SERVES 4

1 quantity of risen pizza dough
 (see opposite)
Flour, for dusting
25g ricotta
2 garlic cloves, crushed
2 tablespoons olive oil
75g Bel Paese, rind removed,
 coarsely chopped
100g mortadella or
 prosciutto, coarsely chopped
A little beaten egg
Vegetable oil for deep-frying
Salt & freshly ground black pepper

Knock back the risen dough, roll it out thinly on a floured surface and cut out eight 15cm rounds.

Mix together the ricotta, garlic, olive oil, Bel Paese and chopped mortadella or prosciutto and season to taste. Put the mixture on one half of each round of dough, leaving a border. Brush the edges of the dough with beaten egg and fold over to make turnovers. Crimp the edges for a neat finish.

Heat the vegetable oil in a large saucepan and fry the calzoni a few at a time for 5–6 minutes, until golden. Alternatively, brush them with a little beaten egg and bake in an oven preheated to 200°C, 400°F, gas 6 for about 12–15 minutes. Serve hot.

To me, these calzoni are lifted out of the ordinary by the inclusion of fennel, a much underrated vegetable which only the Italians seem to use to any extent. Serve the calzoni with a tomato sauce, if you like.

the ultimate vegetarian **calzoni**

SERVES 4

1 quantity of risen pizza dough
(see opposite)
Flour, for dusting
6 tablespoons olive oil
1 garlic clove, crushed
1/4 teaspoon fennel seeds
1 aubergine, peeled & thinly sliced
1 fennel bulb, thinly sliced
150g mozzarella, thinly sliced
10 basil leaves, roughly chopped
A little beaten egg
Vegetable oil for deep-frying
Salt & freshly ground black pepper

Knock back the risen dough, roll it out thinly on a floured surface and cut out eight 15cm rounds.

For the filling, heat the olive oil in a pan with the garlic and fennel seeds. Add the aubergine and fennel and cook gently for 12–15 minutes, until golden and tender. Add a little water to the vegetables if they begin to stick to the pan. Transfer to a bowl and leave to cool, then add the mozzarella and basil. Season to taste, then fill the turnovers, seal with a little beaten egg and cook as in the preceding recipe.

A truly wonderful vegetarian pizza: roasted vegetables topped with contrasting cheeses and drizzled with rosemary oil. A real treat.

roasted vegetable pizza with goat's cheese, **mozzarella** & rosemary oil

SERVES 4

1 red pepper
90ml olive oil
1 courgette, thickly sliced
1 globe artichoke, cooked & cut
  into quarters
8 small, flat mushrooms, stalks
  removed
4 tablespoons tomato passata
12 cherry tomatoes, cut in half
100g goat's cheese, cut
  into 1cm cubes
100g mozzarella, cut
  into 1cm cubes
Salt & freshly ground black pepper

For the dough
2 teaspoons dried yeast
300ml water
450g strong plain flour
1 teaspoon salt
2 tablespoons olive oil
For the rosemary oil
1 garlic clove, crushed
2 tablespoons chopped fresh
  rosemary
90ml extra-virgin olive oil

For the dough, dissolve the yeast in a little of the water. Sift the flour and salt into a bowl and make a well in the centre. Pour the yeast liquid into the well with the remaining water and the olive oil and bring it all together with your hands to form a pliable dough. Knead on a lightly floured surface for 6–8 minutes, until smooth and elastic. Place the dough in a lightly oiled bowl, cover with a damp cloth, then leave at warm room temperature for 1 hour or until doubled in size.

Meanwhile prepare the topping. Preheat the oven to 180°C, 350°F, gas 4. Brush the red pepper with a little of the olive oil, place in a baking dish and roast for 20 minutes. Add the remaining oil to the dish and put the courgette, artichoke and mushrooms in it. Season with salt and pepper and return to the oven for about 25 minutes or until all the vegetables are tender. Remove and leave to cool. Peel the skin off the pepper, cut it in half and remove the seeds. Cut the flesh into strips and set aside.

For the rosemary oil, blitz together the garlic and rosemary with the oil in a blender and set aside.

Raise the oven temperature to 200°C, 400°F, gas 6. Knock back the dough, divide it into 4 pieces and roll out each one into an 18cm circle (or if you're in a party mood, make one big pizza). Spread one quarter of the passata over each pizza base, then top with the roasted vegetables and the halved cherry tomatoes. Scatter both cheeses over the vegetables and drizzle over the rosemary oil. Bake for 15–20 minutes, until golden, then serve straight away.

Dolcelatte and chorizo, a spicy Spanish sausage, make a delicious combination. Add the saltiness and soft texture of oysters and you have a creative and full-flavoured pizza.

oyster & spinach pizza with chorizo sausage & melting **dolcelatte**

SERVES 4

6 tablespoons olive oil
2 red onions, thinly sliced
450g fresh spinach, washed
16 oysters, shucked (see Tip on
  page 30)
1 quantity of risen pizza dough
  (see page 91)
250g chorizo sausage, thinly sliced
175g dolcelatte, crumbled
Salt & freshly ground black pepper

Alternative cheeses
Replace the dolcelatte with some
shaved pecorino or Gruyère or
grated goat's cheese like Rouliabiac
or Duddleswell

Preheat the oven to 200°C, 400°F, gas 6. Heat one third of the oil in a pan, add the onions and fry for 10–12 minutes, until lightly golden. Season and remove from the pan. Heat half the remaining oil in the pan, add the spinach and cook for 2–3 minutes, until wilted. Season with salt and pepper and remove from the pan. Finally, add the rest of the oil to the pan and sauté the oysters for about 1 minute, just enough to seal them. Season and set aside.

Knock back the pizza dough and roll out into four 18cm rounds as in the preceding recipe. Distribute the spinach evenly over each pizza base. Arrange slices of chorizo on top, then dice the oysters and scatter them over. Scatter over the red onions and lastly the crumbled dolcelatte. Bake for 15 minutes or until the cheese is melted and bubbly. Serve straight away.

These little rice fritters are a speciality of Campania, where they are made with mozzarella and known as suppli al telefono, meaning telephone wires, because the molten cheese forms long strings when the fritters are cut open. My version is made with basil and creamy Gorgonzola, so you don't get the stringy effect of the cheese but you do get a wonderful, melting blue cheese fondue in the centre. Serve on a pool of tomato sauce.

suppli alla **gorgonzola** con basilico

SERVES 4

4 tablespoons olive oil
1 onion, finely chopped
1 garlic clove, crushed
250g Arborio rice
500ml Chicken Stock or Cheese-
  infused Chicken Stock (see page 16)
50g unsalted butter
75g Parmesan, freshly grated
A good handful of fresh basil leaves
Freshly grated nutmeg
75g Gorgonzola
3 tablespoons plain flour
2 eggs, beaten
100g fresh white breadcrumbs
Vegetable oil for deep-frying
Salt & freshly ground black pepper

Heat half the olive oil in a heavy-based pan, add the onion and garlic and cook over a gentle heat until tender but not browned. Add the rice and stir well. Heat the stock to simmering point in a separate pan. Add a little of the stock to the rice and stir until it has been absorbed. Keep adding the stock, a ladleful at a time, stirring constantly, until the rice is tender but still firm to the bite. Stir in the butter and Parmesan, then spread the mixture out in a large baking tray and leave to cool.

Put the basil leaves in a blender (reserving a few to garnish the finished dish), add the remaining olive oil and blitz to a thickish purée. Stir the purée into the cooled rice, season to taste with nutmeg, salt and pepper and chill for at least 2 hours, preferably overnight.

To make the suppli, shape the rice mixture into 12–16 balls. Then cut the Gorgonzola into 12–16 pieces and push a piece into the centre of each rice ball. Re-form them neatly, pulling the rice back over the cheese and making sure it is completely enclosed. Coat the rice balls in the flour, then in the beaten egg and finally in the breadcrumbs.

Heat the vegetable oil in a deep-fat fryer or a deep saucepan and fry the suppli in batches for 2–3 minutes, until golden. Drain well on kitchen paper and then serve immediately, garnished with the reserved basil.

PG TIPS
Suppli can also be made with plain boiled rice and can be stuffed with a variety of fillings, one of my favourites being a mixture of sautéed chicken livers, prosciutto and wild mushrooms. For a vegetarian option, try sun-dried tomatoes and sautéed aubergine, and, of course, use vegetable stock instead.

Fonduta is one of Italy's great classic sauces and I use it a lot with pasta and vegetables. Here it makes a creamy addition to an asparagus risotto. Lightly sautéed wild mushrooms can be stirred into the risotto with the asparagus for added flavour, if liked.

asparagus risotto with **fonduta**

SERVES 4

16 asparagus spears, peeled & well
 trimmed
125g unsalted butter
2 shallots, finely diced
250g Arborio rice
600ml Cheese-infused Chicken
 Stock (see page 17)
90ml dry white wine
Salt & freshly ground black pepper

For the fonduta
190g fontina, rind removed,
 thinly sliced
5 tablespoons milk
15g unsalted butter
2 egg yolks
1$^{1}/_{2}$ tablespoons double cream

Alternative cheeses
Beaufort, Jarlsberg, Gruyère,
Emmenthal or Berkswell

For the fonduta, put the cheese in a pan with the milk and leave for 2 hours.

Meanwhile, cook the asparagus in boiling salted water for 5 minutes or until just tender. Drain, refresh in cold water and then dry. Cut into thin diagonal slices and set aside.

Put the butter for the fonduta in a stainless steel or glass bowl set over a pan of gently simmering water, making sure the water does not touch the base of the bowl. When it has melted, add the milk-soaked cheese. Stir until the cheese has melted and the mixture has become more solid. Stir in the egg yolks, one at a time. At this stage the mixture will become runny again. Stir constantly until the sauce has thickened, making sure it does not become too hot or it will curdle. Add the cream and keep warm.

For the risotto, melt 100g of the butter in a saucepan, add the shallots and cook gently until softened but not browned. Add the rice and stir until coated with the butter. Heat the stock to simmering point in a separate pan. Add the white wine and a little of the stock to the rice and stir until the liquid has been absorbed. Keep adding the stock, a ladleful at a time, stirring constantly, until the rice is tender but still retains a bite. Towards the end of cooking, add the stock in smaller quantities and check if the rice is done. It should take about 25 minutes in all.

Add enough of the fonduta to the risotto to give a loose but not sloppy consistency. Melt the remaining butter in a pan and quickly reheat the asparagus in it. Stir the asparagus into the risotto, adjust the seasoning and divide between 4 serving plates. Serve immediately.

PG TIPS
I like asparagus to be well trimmed before cooking. Snap off the white woody part from the base of each spear, then peel away the skin from the base to the bud at the tip. The older and coarser the asparagus, the more trimming it will need.

This is a very good way of using up leftover risotto and in fact it is worth making extra just for this. A crispy fried risotto cake, it makes an ideal accompaniment to a classic osso buco in a rich tomato sauce, or you can serve it with grilled vegetables for a vegetarian dish.

crispy **cheese** risotto al salto

SERVES 4

250g leftover risotto
25g Parmesan, freshly grated
50g fontina or Emmenthal, grated
3 tablespoons vegetable oil
15g unsalted butter, melted
Salt & freshly ground black pepper

Mix the cooked risotto with both cheeses and season well with salt and pepper. Heat a heavy-based frying pan over a high heat. Add the oil and then the rice and cheese mixture, packing it down well to form a cake about 1–2cm thick. Reduce the heat and cook for about 5 minutes, until golden and crisp around the edges. Turn the cake over and cook for a further 5 minutes, until golden and crispy. Turn out on to a serving dish, brush with the melted butter and serve cut into wedges.

Walnuts and nutty-flavoured Gruyère are a great combination and this makes an excellent dish for autumn. For a real treat, sauté some fresh ceps with garlic and parsley, then put them on top of the poached gnocchi before adding the two cheeses.

baked walnut gnocchi with **asiago** & **gruyère**

SERVES 4

350g potatoes (preferably
  King Edward or Maris Piper),
  peeled & cut into chunks
75g walnuts, ground
75g Asiago, grated
15g unsalted butter
2 egg yolks
125g plain flour
Freshly grated nutmeg
Salt & freshly ground black pepper

For the topping
50g unsalted butter
1 tablespoon roughly chopped fresh
  flat-leaf parsley
50g Gruyère, grated
25g Asiago, grated

Cook the potatoes in boiling salted water until tender, then drain well. Mash them while they are still hot. Add the walnuts and Asiago and beat well to allow the cheese to melt. Mix in the butter, egg yolks and half the flour, then season with nutmeg, salt and pepper. Turn the mixture out on to a lightly floured work surface and knead in the remaining flour, a little at a time, to form a smooth, soft but not sloppy dough. Leave to cool.

Roll out the dough into long cylinders 2.5cm thick and cut them into 2cm lengths. Roll each piece over the prongs of a fork to form the classic ridged and slightly curved gnocchi shape. Place the gnocchi on a floured baking tray and leave them to dry for about 1 hour.

Preheat the oven to 180°C, 350°F, gas 4. Poach the gnocchi a few at a time in a large pan of boiling salted water until they rise to the surface, about 2–3 minutes. Remove with a slotted spoon and arrange in a lightly greased, shallow, ovenproof dish.

For the sauce, melt the butter and pour it over the gnocchi, then sprinkle them with the parsley, Gruyère and Asiago. Bake for 12–15 minutes or until the top is brown and crisp. Serve while still bubbling.

The original recipe for these little gnocchi calls for sliced fresh Piedmont truffles – delicious but so expensive! Replace them with white truffle oil which is reasonably priced in comparison and available from specialist delicatessens. If you do happen to get hold of a white truffle, grate it over the top. Malfattini means misshapen, which is appropriate as these are not the usual gnocchi shape. The sauce is a variation of the classic fonduta (see page 96) but uses pecorino instead of fontina.

malfattini of **ricotta** & rocket with **pecorino** & white truffle oil sauce

SERVES 4

25g unsalted butter
175g rocket, plus a few leaves
 to garnish
400g ricotta, sieved
150g plain flour
2 eggs
1 egg yolk
100g Parmesan, freshly
 grated, plus extra to serve
Freshly grated nutmeg
Salt & freshly ground black pepper

For the sauce
150g pecorino Sardo, coarsely grated
50g unsalted butter
50g mascarpone
150ml milk
2 tablespoons white truffle oil

Heat the butter in a pan, add the rocket and cook for 1 minute, until wilted. Leave to cool and then chop finely.

Put the ricotta, flour, eggs and egg yolk in a bowl and mix well together. Stir in the Parmesan and rocket and season with nutmeg, salt and pepper. Shape the mixture into ovals with 2 wet dessertspoons, turning it between them. Drop them in batches into a large pan of lightly simmering salted water and cook until they rise to the surface. Remove with a slotted spoon and drain on kitchen paper. Keep them warm while you make the sauce.

Put the pecorino, butter, mascarpone and milk in a bowl set over a pan of simmering water, making sure the water isn't touching the base of the bowl. Let the cheese melt slowly, whisking occasionally, then whisk in the truffle oil until the mixture comes together into a sauce. Season to taste.

To serve, warm the malfattini through in a low oven for a couple of minutes if necessary, then arrange them in serving bowls. Pour over the sauce, garnish with rocket and sprinkle with a little extra Parmesan.

chapter 5 fish, poultry, meat and game

A simple dish with fresh summer flavours. Caprese is the name given to the famous Italian salad of mozzarella, tomato and basil. Here the tomato and cheese serve as a bed for red mullet, which is scattered liberally with fresh basil leaves. (See the photograph on page 2.)

red mullet on baked salad **caprese** with basil & olive oil

SERVES 4

2 balls of cow's milk mozzarella, cut into slices 1cm thick
8 plum tomatoes, skinned & cut into slices 1cm thick
4 x 175g red mullet fillets, skin on
A small bunch of fresh basil
150ml extra-virgin olive oil
Salt & freshly ground black pepper

Preheat the oven to 220°C, 425°F, gas 7. Lightly oil a shallow ovenproof dish large enough to hold the red mullet fillets in a single layer. Then arrange overlapping alternate slices of mozzarella and tomato over the base of the dish and season with salt and pepper. Lay the mullet fillets on top, skin-side up, season, then scatter over the basil leaves and pour over the olive oil. Bake for 8–10 minutes and then serve immediately.

PG TIPS

I like to serve this dish with some buttery noodles. Sometimes I vary it by adding some diced black olives to the pasta, or even a few sun-dried tomatoes.

Any firm fish would be suitable for this dish. You need to grill the vegetables with the thyme a day in advance and leave them overnight so that their juices run. The juices are then mixed with balsamic vinegar, making a delicious, thyme-scented vinaigrette to drizzle over the fish.

parmesan-crusted sea bass with thyme-grilled vegetables

SERVES 4

75g Parmesan, freshly grated
25g fresh white breadcrumbs
Zest of 1/2 lemon
4 x 175g sea bass fillets, skin on
2 eggs, beaten
4 tablespoons vegetable oil
25g unsalted butter
Salt & freshly ground black pepper

For the vegetables
250g courgettes, cut into
  slices 5mm thick
12 asparagus spears, peeled & well
  trimmed
2 cooked globe artichoke hearts,
  cut into quarters
1 tablespoon fresh thyme leaves
4 tablespoons olive oil
2 tablespoons aged balsamic vinegar

Put the courgettes, asparagus and cooked artichokes on a baking tray, season, then sprinkle over the thyme leaves and toss with the olive oil. Grill over a barbecue (or under a preheated grill) for about 5–6 minutes, until the vegetables are slightly charred all over but still retain a bite. Leave overnight in the refrigerator, covered with cling film.

The next day, drain the juices from the vegetables and reserve. Preheat the oven to 180ºC, 350ºF, gas 4.

Mix together the Parmesan, breadcrumbs, lemon zest and some seasoning. Season the bass fillets on both sides with salt and pepper. Put the beaten eggs in a shallow dish and dip the fish in them to coat both sides, then dip the fish in the Parmesan mixture, pressing it on well.

Reheat the grilled vegetables in the oven. Whisk 3 tablespoons of the reserved cooking juices with the balsamic vinegar.

Heat the oil and butter in a large frying pan until foaming, then add the Parmesan-coated fish fillets. Cook for about 3–4 minutes per side, until golden and crisp. To serve, arrange the thyme-grilled vegetables on serving plates, top with the bass and drizzle around the vinaigrette.

PG TIPS
For variation, rosemary and oregano could replace the thyme, while other good grilling vegetables such as peppers and aubergines could be substituted for the courgettes, asparagus and artichokes. Aged balsamic vinegar is best.

Beurre d'escargot tastes so good that it seems a shame to reserve it for serving with snails. Here it is poured over grilled cod, served on a meltingly rich potato and cheese purée. The smell when it hits the table is something else! I like to accompany this dish with some French beans or grilled leeks.

saffron-grilled cod fillet with aligot & **beurre d'escargot**

SERVES 4

4 tablespoons olive oil
1 tablespoon lemon juice
1/4 teaspoon saffron strands
4 x 150g cod fillets, skin on
1 quantity of freshly prepared Aligot
  (see page 135)
Salt & freshly ground black pepper

For the beurre d'escargot
150g unsalted butter
2 garlic cloves, crushed
3 tablespoons chopped fresh flat-
  leaf parsley, plus a few sprigs
  to garnish
1/4 teaspoon Dijon mustard
2 tablespoons lemon juice

Put the olive oil, lemon juice and saffron in a pan and warm through to infuse the flavours. Pour this over the cod fillets and leave to marinate, either for 2 hours at room temperature or overnight in the refrigerator.

Next prepare the butter, which can be done well ahead of time. Melt the butter over a low heat, then add the garlic. Raise the heat a little and lightly fry the garlic without letting it colour. Stir in the chopped parsley and mustard, then pour into a bowl and leave to cool. Add the lemon juice and season to taste.

To cook the cod, remove it from the marinade, season well and place on a ridged cast-iron grill pan or under a preheated grill. Cook until tender and golden, about 3–4 minutes per side on a grill pan or 5–6 minutes per side under a grill. (You could also fry the fish.)

To serve, put a good dollop of aligot on each serving plate and top with the cod. Reheat the parsley and garlic butter and pour it over the fish, then garnish with sprigs of parsley.

PG TIPS
Another way to serve the fish is to cook it lightly as usual, then to top it with a light mixture of fresh breadcrumbs, mustard and butter and brown it under a hot grill before setting it down on the aligot.

This dish calls for the skate to be enclosed in crépinette (pig's caul), which seals in the filling and keeps the fish moist. A good butcher should be able to get it for you. You will need 4 very thin pieces.

wing of skate with **camembert**, spinach, lardons & cider

SERVES 4

75g streaky bacon in a piece,
  cut into 5mm dice
150g button mushrooms,
  cut into 5mm dice
4 tablespoons crème fraîche
450g spinach, washed
½ small Camembert, cut into
  5mm dice
4 x 300g skate wings
4 pieces of crépinette, about
  25cm square
5 tablespoons dry cider
150ml dry white wine
150ml Chicken Stock (see page 16)
40g unsalted butter, chilled & diced,
  plus a little melted butter
  for brushing
2 tablespoons olive oil
1 tablespoon grainy mustard
Salt & freshly ground black pepper

Alternative cheese
Cooleeney, sometimes known as
Irish Camembert, or Celtic Promise

Preheat the oven to 200°C, 400°F, gas 6. Heat a frying pan until smoking, add the bacon lardons and fry over a high heat until crisp. Add the mushrooms and fry for 2 minutes. Stir in the crème fraîche and cook until reduced by half. Then stir in the spinach, remove from the heat and leave to cool. Add the diced Camembert and some seasoning.

Coat each skate wing with the Camembert and spinach mixture, spreading it evenly with a palette knife. Brush the pieces of crépinette with melted butter, then put the skate on them, stuffing-side down. Wrap the fish well in the crépinette and put it in an ovenproof dish large enough to hold it in a single layer. Pour the cider, wine and chicken stock around the skate and bake for 12–15 minutes, until tender. Remove the fish and keep warm. Strain the juices into a clean pan and whisk in the butter and olive oil a little at a time to form a sauce. Stir in the mustard and adjust the seasoning. Arrange the skate wings on a serving dish, pour over the sauce and serve.

PG TIPS
Other white-fleshed fish such as brill or turbot could replace the skate. Swiss chard or even finely shredded cabbage are good alternatives to the spinach.

Gorwydd Caerphilly has been one of the success stories of British cheese making over the last 2–3 years. Made to a traditional Caerphilly recipe, which had all but disappeared, it is a wonderful cheese with the crumbly characteristics we have come to know and love. It is very versatile for cooking and here is one of my favourite ways to enjoy it.

braised halibut with **gorwydd caerphilly** crust, spinach & tomatoes

SERVES 4

4 x 160g skinless & boneless
  halibut fillets
100ml fish stock
50ml dry white wine
150g plum tomatoes, cut
  into quarters
1 tablespoon olive oil
2 tablespoons Dijon mustard
25g unsalted butter
500g fresh spinach leaves

For the cheese crust
75g fresh white breadcrumbs
50g Gorwydd Caerphilly cheese,
  finely grated
50g unsalted butter softened
4 tablespoons chopped fresh
  basil leaves
2 tablespoons chopped fresh
  tarragon leaves

Alternative cheeses
Cheddar or Emmental

For the crust, place all the ingredients together in a blender and blend until smooth. Spread the mixture out onto a baking tray lined with clingfilm and press down so that there are no gaps. Place in the fridge for about 30 minutes to set .

Preheat the oven to 200ºC, 400ºF, mark 6. Place the halibut fillets in a large baking tray. Pour over the white wine and fish stock and season well with salt and pepper. Brush the top of the fish liberally with mustard.

Cut the cheese crust into 4 with a knife to fit the top of each fish and lay on top of the fillets. Place in the hot oven, uncovered, and cook for 7–8 minutes or until cooked through.

Meanwhile, heat the butter in a frying pan, add the tomatoes and spinach and sauté for 2 minutes until wilted. Season to taste.

Place a pile of the spinach and tomato mixture on 4 individual serving plates, top each with the cheese-crusted halibut and serve.

PG TIPS
New potatoes make a lovely, simple accompaniment, but I often like to serve with some creamy oven-baked gratin potatoes.

Sardines have become newly fashionable over the past few years, and, what's more, they're good for us and very reasonably priced. This Parmesan, fennel and lemon stuffing goes nicely with them. Mackerel can be used instead of sardines, if you prefer.

stuffed sardines with **parmesan** gremolata & caper butter

SERVES 4

24 fresh sardines, about 15cm
  long, scaled
4 tablespoons olive oil
2 garlic cloves, crushed
1 fennel bulb, with its green feathery
  leaves, finely chopped
1 tablespoon chopped fresh thyme
1 tablespoon chopped fresh oregano
Zest of 1 lemon
1 tablespoon Pernod or other
  aniseed liqueur
25g fresh white breadcrumbs
50g Parmesan, freshly grated
Freshly grated nutmeg
Salt & freshly ground black pepper

For the caper butter
125g unsalted butter
2 shallots, finely chopped
3 tablespoons superfine capers,
  rinsed & drained
1 tablespoon chopped fresh parsley
Juice of 1 lemon

Alternative cheeses
Grana padana (a cheaper version of
Parmesan), Asiago, pecorino or 'Dry
Aged Jack' (USA)

Preheat the oven to 200°C, 400°F, gas 6. Slit the sardines open along the belly and carefully pull out the entrails. Open the fish flat and carefully pull out the backbone from the head to the tail, snipping it off at the tail end with scissors and leaving the head and tail intact. Set the fish aside.

Heat half the oil in a pan, add the garlic and cook gently until tender. Add the fennel and cook for 5 minutes. Then stir in the herbs, lemon zest and Pernod, followed by the breadcrumbs and Parmesan. Season to taste with nutmeg, salt and pepper and remove from the heat.

Fill the cavity of each sardine with this mixture, pressing it in well. Put the fish on an oiled baking sheet, brush them with the remaining oil and bake for 8–10 minutes, until cooked through.

For the caper butter, melt the butter over a low heat, then add the shallots, capers and parsley. Cook until the butter begins to foam and becomes nutty in fragrance. Add the lemon juice, then immediately pour the butter over the sardines and serve.

This is based on that great dish, lobster Thermidor. All you need to serve with it is a simple rice pilaff.

gratin of lobster with **parmesan** & tarragon sauce

SERVES 4

4 cooked lobsters, weighing about 500g each
25g unsalted butter
Cayenne pepper, to taste
5 tablespoons dry white wine
1 tablespoon chopped fresh tarragon, plus a few sprigs to garnish
300ml Basic Cheese Sauce (see page 18)
4 tablespoons double cream, semi-whipped
3 tablespoons freshly grated Parmesan
Salt & freshly ground black pepper

Cut the claws off the lobster with a large knife, then split the lobster in half down the back: the easiest way to do this is to put a large knife through the centre of the body section and cut down through the head, then take out the knife, turn the lobster round and cut down the centre of the body through the tail. Remove and discard the head sac and the intestinal vein, then take out the lobster meat from the head and tail and cut it into large cubes. Discard the gills (known as 'dead men's fingers') from the lobster shells and reserve the shells. Crack the claws in 2 or 3 places and pick out the meat.

Heat the butter in a pan, add the lobster meat and season with salt, pepper and cayenne. Pour in the white wine, bring to the boil and simmer for 1 minute – no longer or the lobster will toughen. Remove the lobster from the pan with a slotted spoon and continue to boil the wine until it is reduced by half its volume. Stir in the chopped tarragon and the cheese sauce, then fold in the cream and return the lobster to the pan. Adjust the seasoning.

Fill the 8 lobster shells with the sauce, put them on a baking sheet or in a shallow gratin dish and sprinkle with the grated Parmesan. Brown under a hot grill and then serve, garnished with sprigs of tarragon.

Manchego is Spain's best-known cheese and, when fresh, has a mild, creamy consistency. Many Spanish recipes begin with instructions to prepare a sofrito – onions, garlic, tomatoes and sometimes parsley, cooked slowly to make a thick, intensely flavoured savoury base. This particular dish is of Mexican-Spanish origin and could be made with almost any seafood. Try lobster or scallops for an extravagant version. Saffron rice makes a good accompaniment.

sizzling prawns with sofrito, peppers & **manchego**

SERVES 4

4 tablespoons olive oil
50g unsalted butter
2 garlic cloves, crushed
20–24 large raw prawns, shelled &
  deveined
1 red onion, cut into wedges about
  5mm thick
2 red peppers, halved, deseeded &
  cut into strips 1cm wide
1 green pepper, halved, deseeded &
  cut into strips 1cm wide
300g tomatoes, skinned,
  deseeded & chopped
A pinch of cayenne pepper
$1/2$ teaspoon paprika
250g Manchego, cut into 2cm cubes
2 tablespoons fresh coriander leaves
Salt & freshly ground black pepper

Alternative cheese
Feta or 'Dry Aged Jack' (US)

Heat the oil and butter in a frying pan until the butter is foaming, then add the garlic and cook for 1 minute. Throw in the prawns and sauté them over a fairly high heat for about 1–2 minutes, until coloured. Remove from the pan and keep warm. Add the onion and peppers to the pan, cover and cook over a low heat for 15 minutes, until softened.

Stir in the tomatoes, cayenne and paprika and cook for about 5 minutes, until the tomatoes begin to break down. Return the prawns to the pan, stir together, then add the Manchego and sauté for 30 seconds. Season to taste, scatter over the fresh coriander and serve immediately.

I think that it's fair to say that most cheese dishes simply include a little cheese rather than use it as the main ingredient. One exception is fondue, a dish invented in the Swiss Alps to use the famous cheeses of the region, Emmenthal and Gruyère. My favourite fondue combines Emmenthal with Camembert from Normandy for a tasty modern variation. It is very important to have a proper fondue pot. This is easy to find and well worth a small investment in order to keep your fondue at the right temperature.

mussel **fondue** normandie

SERVES 6 AS A STARTER,
4 AS A MAIN COURSE

225g Emmenthal, grated
1 tablespoon cornflour
$\frac{1}{2}$ garlic clove
300ml dry white wine
250g very ripe Camembert, rind
  removed, cut into small pieces
6 tablespoons dry cider
Freshly grated nutmeg
Salt & freshly ground black pepper

For the mussels
900g mussels
1 shallot, finely chopped
A few parsley stalks
175ml dry white wine

First clean the mussels. Scrub them under cold running water, pulling out their 'beards' and scraping off any barnacles with a knife. Discard any open mussels that do not close when tapped lightly on a work surface.

For the fondue, gently toss the Emmenthal with the cornflour and set aside. Rub the inside of a fondue pot or earthenware casserole with the cut surface of the garlic. Pour in the white wine and cook over a low heat until it just starts to bubble. Gradually stir in the Emmenthal and keep stirring until smooth. Then add the Camembert and blend together until the Camembert melts and the mixture is smooth again. Add the cider, season with salt, pepper and nutmeg, and keep warm.

Place the mussels in a pan with the shallot, parsley stalks and white wine, cover with a tight-fitting lid and place over a high heat, shaking the pan once or twice, until the mussels have opened (about 3–4 minutes). Drain them in a colander, reserving the cooking liquid, and discard any mussels that remain closed. Remove the mussels from their shells and keep warm. Strain the cooking liquid and add to the fondue. Serve the mussels with fondue forks to dip into the Camembert fondue.

PG TIPS
Any seafood would be good instead of mussels. I sometimes serve the fondue with new potatoes: dip them into the pot too – delicious!

The classic combination of mozzarella, tomato and basil in a different guise. You can use turbot or a similar white fish instead of chicken and it works just as well. Tomato tapenade is now available in jars in many supermarkets but I still think that home-made is better. Besides, it's really quick to make your own. You won't need to use all of it in this recipe but it keeps well in the refrigerator.

chicken schnitzel with **mozzarella**, tomato tapenade & basil

SERVES 4

4 x 150g skinless & boneless
  chicken breasts
Flour, for dusting
1 egg, beaten
4 tablespoons fresh white
  breadcrumbs
4 tablespoons olive oil
100g unsalted butter
1 ball of mozzarella, cut into 8 slices
2 tablespoons roughly chopped fresh
  basil
Juice of 1/2 lemon
Salt & freshly ground black pepper

For the tomato tapenade
75g sun-dried tomatoes
25g superfine capers, rinsed
  & drained
2 garlic cloves, crushed
4 tablespoons oil from the
  sun-dried tomatoes

For the tapenade, put all the ingredients in a blender and blitz to a coarse purée (do not purée it too finely or it will become mushy).

Put the chicken breasts between 2 sheets of cling film and beat lightly with a meat mallet or the end of a rolling pin until they are just under 5mm thick. Season with salt and pepper, then dust lightly with flour. Dip them in the beaten egg and then in the breadcrumbs. Brush off any excess crumbs.

Heat the olive oil and 25g butter in a frying pan and add the chicken. Cook for about 4–5 minutes on each side, until the chicken is golden and cooked through, then transfer to heatproof serving plates. Top each chicken breast with 2 slices of mozzarella, then spread 1/2 tablespoon of tomato tapenade over the cheese. Place under a hot grill until the mozzarella begins to soften.

Meanwhile, heat the remaining butter in a frying pan until it is foaming and smells nutty. Add the basil and lemon juice, pour it over the chicken and serve immediately.

PG TIPS
Sometimes I make this with tomato tapenade spread over one slice of mozzarella and black olive tapenade on the other. The contrast of black, red and white looks spectacular. (Olive tapenade is available in jars in most supermarkets.)

I recently discovered spatchcocked poussins in a major supermarket. What a superb idea! All the work has been done for you. If you are not lucky enough to find them, don't be too alarmed at the thought of preparing the birds yourself. After a few attempts you'll wonder what all the fuss was about. Your guests will be impressed too. Serve the chickens with a watercress salad and new potatoes.

grilled chicken spatchcock with **tomme, ricotta verde & sweet shallot vinaigrette**

SERVES 4

4 x 400g poussins, free-range
 if possible
75g white Tomme
75g ricotta
1 bunch of watercress, stalks
removed, leaves finely chopped
2 tablespoons chopped fresh basil
1 shallot, finely chopped
1 garlic clove, crushed
2 tablespoons olive oil
Lemon wedges, to serve
Salt & freshly ground black pepper

For the marinade
1 garlic clove, crushed
Juice & zest of 2 lemons
4 tablespoons olive oil

For the vinaigrette
4 shallots, finely sliced
10g unsalted butter
A pinch of sugar
1 tablespoon champagne vinegar
4 tablespoons olive oil
1/2 teaspoon Dijon mustard

To spatchcock the poussins, you simply need to open them out flat. To do this, cut out the backbone with kitchen scissors or poultry shears. Break the wishbone, then turn each bird cut-side down and flatten it by pressing down with the heel of your hand. Turn it over and remove all the ribcage bones.

Mix together all the ingredients for the marinade, season with salt and pepper and pour into a large shallow container – you might need 2 to hold the poussins. Add the poussins, turning them to coat, cover and leave to marinate for at least 4 hours, but preferably overnight, in the refrigerator.

To make the vinaigrette, gently fry the shallots in the butter with the sugar until golden and lightly caramelized. Whisk together the vinegar, oil, mustard and some salt and pepper. Add the hot shallots and leave to cool. (This can be done several hours in advance.)

In a bowl, mix together the Tomme, ricotta, watercress, basil, shallot, garlic and olive oil. Season to taste. Remove the poussins from the marinade and dry well. Carefully loosen the skin of each bird without detaching it and push the stuffing underneath, spreading it over the flesh – it's easiest to use your fingers. Smooth the skin over again and season with salt and pepper.

Grill the poussins for about 7–8 minutes on each side, until tender and cooked through. A charcoal grill would be ideal but you could use a ridged grill pan instead, or fry them. Put them on warmed serving plates, drizzle over a little of the vinaigrette and serve the rest on the side. Accompany with lemon wedges.

PG TIPS
If you find it difficult removing the ribcage from the raw poussins, take out the bones after the birds have been cooked. They will come away much more easily.

This may seem rather an unusual combination but, if you think about it, grapes are invariably served on a cheeseboard and they are also often cooked with quails. This recipe brings all three ingredients together. Muscat grapes are recommended for their exceptional sweetness but the dish also works well with red grapes. Serve with artichoke hearts or French beans that have been sautéed in butter with bacon and onions. If you don't manage to get hold of quails, you could use 4 poussins instead, in which case you would need to double the amount of stuffing.

quails stuffed with **sage derby** & muscat grapes

SERVES 4

8 quails, boned (ask your butcher to do this & give you the bones, if possible)
100g softened unsalted butter
100g Sage Derby, grated
1 shallot, finely chopped
1 small garlic clove, crushed
Salt & freshly ground black pepper

For the sauce
90ml white wine
300ml Reduced Meat Stock (see page 17)
350g muscat grapes
3 tablespoons Muscat de Beaumes de Venise or vin de Jura

Alternative cheeses
Dolcelatte would be ideal. Even a stronger blue such as Stilton or Roquefort would work well or you could use a milder Cornish Blue

Preheat the oven to 220°C, 425°F, gas 7. Season the quails inside and out. Prepare the stuffing by beating together 75g butter, the Sage Derby, shallot, garlic and a little seasoning. Stuff the quails with this mixture and seal them by pulling the skin over the opening and securing with a cocktail stick. Place in a small roasting tin. Melt the remaining butter and brush it over the quails, then roast for 12–15 minutes, until juicy and tender and still slightly pink. Remove from the roasting tin and keep warm.

For the sauce, put the quail bones in the roasting tin, place it on the hob and fry until the bones are golden brown. Add the white wine and bring to the boil, stirring to scrape up the sediment from the base of the tin. Simmer for 2 minutes, until the wine has evaporated. Pour in the meat stock and bring to the boil, skimming off any impurities from the surface. Reduce the heat and simmer for 10 minutes.

Meanwhile pass half the grapes through a centrifugal juice extractor. When the sauce has reduced and thickened to a light, syrupy consistency, strain it through a sieve into a clean pan, add the Beaumes de Venise or vin de Jura and the fresh grape juice. Simmer for 2 minutes, then add the remaining grapes to the sauce and reheat until boiling. Adjust the seasoning to taste.

Return the quails to the oven for 2 minutes to reheat them, then put them on 4 serving plates. Pour the sauce around the quails and serve.

PG TIPS
If you do not have a centrifugal juice extractor, purée the grapes in a liquidizer, then sieve them. If seedless grapes are unavailable, deseed them by using a clean hair grip or by cutting them in half and removing the seeds.

I often serve this winter-inspired dish around Christmas time, garnished with baby roasted onions and glazed chestnuts – delicious! Pheasant has a tendency to be dry if not cooked with care. By wrapping the breasts in smoked bacon you can keep them moist and tender.

roast breast of pheasant wrapped in smoked bacon with caraway cabbage & **gorgonzola** polenta

SERVES 4

4 pheasant breasts, bones removed
 & chopped
8 smoked bacon rashers
4 tablespoons vegetable oil
75g unsalted butter
1 Savoy cabbage, central core
 removed, finely shredded
1 teaspoon caraway seeds
300ml water
Freshly grated nutmeg
1/2 quantity of Gorzonzola Polenta
 (see page 132)
Salt & freshly ground black pepper

For the sauce
3 shallots, roughly chopped
1 garlic clove, roughly chopped
1 sprig of fresh thyme
1 bay leaf
6 juniper berries, lightly crushed
6 black peppercorns, lightly crushed
5 tablespoons red wine vinegar
150ml red wine
150ml Meat Stock (see page 17)
4 tablespoons port
1/2 tablespoon redcurrant jelly

Preheat the oven to 220°C, 425°F, gas 7. Season the pheasant breasts all over with salt and pepper, then wrap each one in 2 overlapping rashers of bacon. Secure with a cocktail stick. Heat half the oil and butter in an ovenproof frying pan or shallow casserole dish until foaming, then add the pheasant breasts and fry briefly until browned all over. Transfer to the oven and roast for 8–10 minutes, until tender.

Meanwhile, heat the remaining oil in a saucepan and cook the cabbage over a low heat until it begins to wilt. Add the remaining butter, the caraway seeds and water. Bring to the boil and cook until the cabbage is tender and all the liquid has evaporated. Then season with salt, pepper and a little nutmeg and keep warm.

Remove the pheasant breasts from the oven and take out the cocktail sticks. Keep the pheasant warm while you make the sauce. Put the chopped pheasant bones, shallots, garlic, thyme, bay leaf, juniper berries and peppercorns in the pan in which the pheasant was cooked and fry gently for 2–3 minutes, until golden. Pour in the vinegar and boil for 1 minute, stirring to scrape up the sediment from the base of the pan. Add the red wine and boil until the liquid has reduced by half its volume. Next add the stock and boil until reduced by a third. Stir in the port and redcurrant jelly and adjust the seasoning. Strain through a fine sieve.

To serve, reheat the polenta if necessary. Arrange the cabbage on 4 warmed serving plates and place the pheasant on top. Garnish with a large scoop of polenta and pour the sauce around.

This recipe sounds like a contradiction in terms, since the whole point of steak tartare is that it is served raw. But what I've done is taken the ingredients for steak tartare – best-quality minced beef, Worcestershire sauce, onions, capers, mustard and egg yolk – and put them together into a hamburger, with the added bonus of delicious, melting Roquefort cheese in the centre. Serve with good chunky chips and a crisp green salad.

grilled steak tartare with **roquefort**

SERVES 4

750g best-quality minced beef
2 tablespoons Worcestershire sauce
1 onion, very finely chopped
1 tablespoon superfine capers,
  rinsed, drained & chopped
1 tablespoon chopped fresh parsley
1 tablespoon Dijon mustard
1 egg yolk
150g Roquefort, crumbled
Salt & freshly ground black pepper

Alternative cheeses
For a different flavour entirely,
substitute goat's cheese or
Emmenthal for the Roquefort

Mix the beef, Worcestershire sauce, onion, capers, parsley and mustard together in a bowl. Season with salt and pepper, then stir in the egg yolk. Chill for about 30 minutes, until firm.

Divide the mixture into 4 balls. With your thumb, make an indentation in each one and fill with the Roquefort. Pull the meat back over the cheese until it is completely covered. Flatten into hamburgers, season lightly, then barbecue, grill or fry them.

This is a good dish for a barbecue as it can be put together very easily. However, if it rains, you can always grill or fry the steaks indoors.

pepper-crusted rib eye of beef with **roquefort** butter, sautéed potatoes & porcini mushrooms

SERVES 4

450g new potatoes
4 tablespoons olive oil
200g fresh porcini mushrooms, thinly sliced
2 tablespoons roughly chopped fresh sage
4 x 275g rib eye of beef steaks, well trimmed
2 tablespoons coarsely ground black peppercorns
1/2 quantity of Roquefort Butter (see page 19)
Salt

Cook the potatoes in boiling salted water until just tender, then drain and leave until cool enough to handle. Peel and cut into slices 1cm thick. Heat the oil in a frying pan, add the potatoes and sauté until golden and tender. Add the porcini and sage and sauté until the mushrooms are tender. Season with salt and pepper and keep warm.

Coat the rib eye steaks evenly with the coarsely ground peppercorns and season with a little salt. Cook on a barbecue until done to your liking.

Arrange the potatoes on 4 serving plates, top with the steaks and put a pat of Roquefort butter on top of each steak. Serve immediately. The delicate cheese butter will melt on its way to the table.

PG TIPS

If you can't get fresh porcini mushrooms, use chestnut mushrooms instead. This simple recipe lends itself to many adaptations – for instance, lamb or pork cutlets, or a rump steak. The cheese butter is an ideal way to use up scraps of cheese.

This dish evolved from the French classic, steak Bordelaise, which is beef in a red wine sauce with bone marrow. In my adaptation the marrow is topped with shaved Parmesan and the sauce enriched with aged balsamic vinegar. I generally serve it with buttered spinach with porcini mushrooms and pan-roasted shallots alongside, but any green vegetable would be good.

fillet of beef with bone marrow & **parmesan** crostini & red wine balsamic vinegar jus

SERVES 4

4 x 175g fillet steaks, well trimmed (cut the trimmings into small pieces & save for the sauce)
3 tablespoons vegetable oil
100g mixed vegetables, such as onion, leek & carrot, finely diced
200ml red wine
4 tablespoons aged balsamic vinegar
300ml Reduced Meat Stock (see page 17)
8 large slices of beef bone marrow (see Tip)
4 x 7.5cm round bread croûtes, toasted
25g fresh Parmesan, cut into shavings
Salt & freshly ground black pepper

Alternative cheese
Asiago

Season the steaks with salt and pepper. Heat the oil in a large heavy-based frying pan until smoking. Fry the steaks quickly on both sides so that they turn a beautiful rich dark colour, then cook until they are done to your liking: 2–3 minutes per side for rare, 5–6 for medium. Remove from the pan and keep warm in a low oven. Add the meat trimmings to the pan, together with the mixed vegetables, and fry until golden. Pour in the red wine and balsamic vinegar and bring to the boil, stirring to scrape up the sediment from the base of the pan. Boil for 5 minutes, then pour in the stock and simmer until it has thickened slightly and become syrupy; it should be thick enough to coat the back of a spoon. Taste and adjust the seasoning if necessary.

Meanwhile, poach the slices of marrow in a little salted water or, better still, meat stock for 1 minute, then drain. Put 2 slices of poached marrow on each croûte and cover with the shaved Parmesan. Put the steaks on warm serving plates, top each one with a marrow crostini and pour around the red wine sauce. Grind some black pepper over the top and serve.

PG TIPS
You will have to go to a good old-fashioned butcher's shop to get hold of bone marrow. A very co-operative butcher might extract the marrow from the bone for you. If not, ask for bones cut into 7.5cm lengths and then poach them for 1–2 minutes. This will enable you to scoop out the marrow easily.

A cheese rarebit is a peculiarly English dish that dates back at least to the time of Shakespeare. I came across this 18th-century recipe for blue cheese rarebit in an old cookery book. I like to make it with one of my favourite cheeses, Scottish Dunsyre Blue.

veal steaks with **blue cheese** rarebit, roasted celeriac & rosemary sauce

SERVES 4

675g celeriac, peeled &
  cut into batons 10 x 2 x 2cm
90ml vegetable oil
200g Dunsyre Blue, finely diced
2 teaspoons mustard
100ml light beer
4 x 150g veal fillet steaks
  (or veal chops)
Salt & freshly ground black pepper

For the sauce
25g unsalted butter
2 shallots, finely chopped
1 tablespoon chopped fresh
  rosemary
150ml red wine
450ml Reduced Meat Stock
  (see page 17)

Alternative cheeses
Any blue such as Stilton,
Beenleigh Blue, Bleu des Causses
or Y-Fenni

Preheat the oven to 200°C, 400°F, gas 6. Blanch the celeriac batons in boiling salted water for 2–3 minutes, then drain well in a colander. Place on a baking tray, toss with half the oil and bake for 20–25 minutes, until golden.

Meanwhile, for the rarebit, put the cheese, mustard and beer in a pan over a low heat, stirring constantly, until the cheese melts; the mixture should be the consistency of thickish cream. Season with pepper and keep warm.

Heat the remaining oil in a frying pan, season the steaks and fry for about 3–5 minutes on each side. Remove from the pan and keep warm.

For the sauce, add the butter, shallots and rosemary to the pan in which the veal was cooked and fry until the shallots are lightly golden. Pour in the red wine and boil for 2–3 minutes, then add the meat stock. Boil until reduced and thickened to a saucelike consistency, then strain through a fine sieve.

Spread the blue cheese rarebit over the veal steaks and place under a hot grill for 2–3 minutes, until the rarebit has turned golden and bubbly. Transfer to serving plates, pour the sauce around and garnish with the roasted celeriac.

My new-look saltimbocca uses all the elements of one of Italy's classic dishes, with the addition of thinly sliced fontina and a light Parmesan crust. In spring, asparagus tips and baby leeks make good accompaniments.

new-look **saltimbocca**

SERVES 4

4 x 200g thin veal escalopes
4 slices of prosciutto
8 thin slices of fontina, rind removed
Flour, for dusting
3 eggs, beaten
75g Parmesan, freshly grated
50g fresh white breadcrumbs
4 tablespoons vegetable oil or
   clarified butter (see Tip on page 83)
2 lemons, peel & pith removed, cut
   into slices 5mm thick
Salt & freshly ground black pepper

For the sauce
300ml Reduced Meat Stock
   (see page 17)
4 tablespoons Marsala wine
75g unsalted butter
20 small fresh sage leaves
2 tablespoons lemon juice

Alternative cheeses
Port Salut or Fontal

The veal escalopes should be no more than 3mm thick. If necessary, put them between 2 sheets of cling film and flatten with a meat mallet or a rolling pin. Season the escalopes with salt and pepper. Lay a slice of prosciutto on top of each one, then 2 slices of fontina. Fold up the edges of the veal to enclose the filling. Season again, then dust lightly with flour and chill for 30 minutes.

For the sauce, bring the stock and Marsala to the boil and simmer until it forms a light sauce consistency.

Beat together the eggs, Parmesan and breadcrumbs and add a little seasoning. Heat the oil or clarified butter in a large frying pan, dip each veal escalope into the egg and cheese mixture to coat, then fry for about 5 minutes on each side, until golden and cooked through. Transfer to a warm serving dish, top each escalope with 2 slices of lemon and pour the Marsala sauce around. Heat the butter until it is foaming and gives off a nutty aroma. Add the sage leaves and lemon juice and then pour over the veal. Serve immediately.

PG TIPS
It can be difficult judging the correct consistency of a sauce. If it seems too thin, reduce it by boiling until it has thickened enough to coat the back of a spoon.

A creamy potato purée or some soft or grilled polenta would go well with the chargrilled lamb and sautéed red peppers in this dish.

chargrilled lamb cutlets with coriander & **goat's cheese** pesto & peppers

SERVES 4

90ml olive oil
2 garlic cloves, crushed
1 small red chilli
4 red peppers, deseeded
1 tablespoon white wine vinegar
8 thickly cut lamb cutlets (or chops)
1/2 quantity of Coriander & Goat's
  Cheese Pesto (see page 20)
Salt & freshly ground black pepper

Heat the olive oil in a frying pan, add the garlic and the whole chilli and cook for 1 minute over a low heat to infuse the oil. Cut the peppers into strips 1cm wide and add to the pan, season with salt and pepper and then sauté for 3–4 minutes. Add a little water, cover and cook over a low heat for 10–15 minutes, until tender. Uncover the pan, raise the heat and cook until all the liquid has evaporated. Add the vinegar and cook until that, too, has evaporated. Remove the chilli and adjust the seasoning. Keep warm.

Season the lamb cutlets and cook them on a ridged grill pan until they are done to your liking. Arrange the peppers on 4 plates, top with the lamb cutlets, then spoon over the pesto and serve.

Lamb shanks are becoming popular because they are tasty and very good value for money. Here they are served with Greek ingredients – oregano, feta, lemon and olive oil – to make a hearty, satisfying dish.

lamb shanks with **feta**, anchovy & braised chickpeas

SERVES 6

1 tablespoon anchovy fillets, rinsed
2 tablespoons grated lemon zest
2 tablespoons chopped fresh oregano
4 tablespoons olive oil
2 garlic cloves, crushed
6 small lamb shanks, trimmed
175g Greek feta
Salt & freshly ground black pepper

For the chickpeas
2 tablespoons olive oil
1 onion, finely chopped
1/2 tablespoon ground cumin
1 teaspoon turmeric
225g dried chickpeas, soaked
  overnight & then drained
4 tomatoes, skinned & chopped
300ml passata

For the chickpeas, heat the oil in a pan, add the onion, cumin and turmeric and sweat until the onion is tender. Add the chickpeas, cover with water and bring to the boil. Reduce the heat and simmer for 1 hour, or until the chickpeas are tender. About 10 minutes before the end of cooking, add the chopped tomatoes and passata to form a thick sauce around the chickpeas. Season to taste.

Finely chop the anchovy fillets and mix together with the lemon zest, oregano, oil and garlic to make a paste. Rub the paste all over the lamb shanks. Leave to marinate for up to 2 hours at room temperature.

Grill the lamb on a barbecue or a ridged cast-iron grill pan for 10–12 minutes on each side (this gives pink lamb), or until done to your liking.

Meanwhile, reheat the braised chickpeas and arrange on serving plates. Top with the lamb and coarsely grate the feta over the top. Serve immediately.

chapter 6 **vegetable dishes**

Leeks and bacon make a wonderful marriage of flavours. With the addition of Red Leicester cheese, this simple gratin reaches new heights. It makes an ideal accompaniment to a good Sunday roast.

gratin of leeks with **red leicester** & smoked bacon

SERVES 4

A pinch of sugar
8 medium leeks
15g unsalted butter
1 tablespoon plain flour
300ml Vegetable Stock (see page 16)
  or semi-skimmed milk
1 teaspoon Dijon mustard
90ml double cream
100g Red Leicester, grated
50g smoked bacon, rind
  removed, coarsely chopped
Salt & freshly ground black pepper

Bring a pan of water to the boil with the sugar and some salt. Plunge the leeks into the water and simmer for 8–10 minutes, until just tender. Remove and drain well, then dry on a cloth.

Melt the butter in a pan, stir in the flour and cook over a gentle heat for 1–2 minutes. Gradually add the stock or milk and bring to the boil, stirring constantly. Reduce the heat and cook very gently for 10 minutes. Remove from the heat and stir in the mustard, cream and half the cheese, then season to taste. Arrange the leeks in a gratin dish, season and coat with the sauce.

In a hot frying pan, sauté the bacon until crisp. Drain and scatter it over the leeks. Finally sprinkle over the remaining cheese. Place under a hot grill for a few minutes until bubbling and golden. Serve straight away.

I find this creamy blue cheese polenta far superior to the plain variety finished with Parmesan.

soft **gorgonzola** polenta with young spinach & wild mushrooms

SERVES 4–6

25g unsalted butter
150g mixed wild mushrooms,
  such as ceps, chanterelles & oyster
  mushrooms, halved if large
90ml Madeira or port
300ml Meat Stock (see page 17)
2 tablespoons olive oil
100g young spinach leaves, washed
Freshly grated nutmeg
1 tablespoon chopped fresh chives,
  to garnish
Salt & freshly ground black pepper

For the polenta
2 litres water
2 teaspoons salt
100g unsalted butter
350g polenta
150g Gorgonzola, crumbled

Alternative cheeses
Bleu de Bresse, Blue Castello (AUS)
or Yorkshire Blue

For the polenta, bring the water, salt and butter to the boil in a large pan. Slowly rain in the polenta, stirring all the time. Simmer over a gentle heat for 30–35 minutes, stirring very frequently, until cooked; the polenta should be pulling away from the sides of the pan. Remove from the heat, stir in the Gorgonzola and allow it to melt. The polenta should be quite soft and smooth in texture. Adjust the seasoning and keep warm.

Heat the butter in a pan and fry the wild mushrooms over a high heat until tender. Remove the mushrooms from the pan and set aside. Pour in the Madeira or port and stock and boil until the liquid has reduced by half. Season to taste, return the mushrooms to the pan and keep warm.

Heat the olive oil in a pan, add the spinach and cook until just wilted, then season with nutmeg, salt and pepper.

To serve, pour the polenta into 4 warmed shallow bowls, place the spinach in the centre, then arrange the mushrooms on top. Garnish with the chives.

Some people find the idea of cooking a soufflé too daunting to contemplate, but as long as you follow the rules it can be a very simple dish to add to your repertoire. Here is one of my personal favourites. A delicious variation for any cheese soufflé is to put some diced cheese in the centre of the mixture when you are filling the dish. It will melt as the soufflé cooks, resulting in a wonderful fondue-like texture.

aubergine & **roquefort** soufflé

SERVES 6

15g Parmesan, freshly grated
125ml olive oil
3 medium aubergines, peeled & cut
 into small cubes
150ml water
A good pinch of paprika
75g Roquefort
40g unsalted butter, plus extra
 for greasing
40g plain flour
250ml milk, boiled & strained
4 egg yolks
6 egg whites
Salt & freshly ground black pepper

Alternative cheeses
Bleu d'Auvergne, Lanark Blue,
Oregon Blue (US) or Meredith Blue
(AUS)

Butter six 200ml soufflé dishes or one 1.2 litre soufflé dish and dust them with the Parmesan, turning the dishes to coat them evenly. Tip out any excess cheese.

Preheat the oven to 230°C, 450°F, gas 8. Heat the olive oil in a large frying pan, add the aubergines and fry until lightly golden. Don't crowd the pan: you may have to cook them in batches. Return all the aubergines to the pan, add the water, then cover and cook over a gentle heat for up to 30 minutes, stirring occasionally, until the aubergines are very soft and fairly dry in texture. Put them in a blender with a little salt, some pepper and the paprika. To this add 50g of the Roquefort and blitz to a smooth, thickish purée. Set aside.

Heat the butter in a pan, add the flour and cook over a low heat for a few minutes. Gradually add the hot milk, stirring all the time, then bring to the boil to make a smooth sauce. Cook over a very low heat for about 5 minutes, then stir in the aubergine and Roquefort purée. Leave to cool slightly before stirring in the egg yolks.

Whisk the egg whites until they form stiff peaks. Beat a third of the whites into the sauce to loosen the mixture, then carefully fold in the remaining whites. Half fill the soufflé dishes with the mixture and crumble the remaining Roquefort over the top. Pour over the remaining soufflé mixture and wipe any drips off the rims of the dishes. Place on a baking sheet and bake for 20 minutes, until all the soufflés are well risen and nicely golden. Serve immediately.

PG TIPS

For successful soufflé making: Ensure that the bowl in which you whisk the egg whites is clean and grease free; rub it with a little lemon, then rinse under cold water and dry on a clean cloth. Do not overbeat the egg whites or they will become grainy. Be careful not to leave fingerprints along the rim of the soufflé dish or the soufflé will not rise evenly. Soufflés must be served immediately. Remember: 'The guests should wait for the soufflé and not the other way round!'

Aligot is a peasant dish from the Auvergne region of France and makes hearty and sustaining cold-weather fare. In some areas garlic is traditionally included. It's very good served with sausages, braised meat or even, less conventionally, with fish – see the recipe for Saffron-grilled Cod Fillet with Aligot and Beurre d'Escargot on page 104.

aligot (cheese & potato purée)

SERVES 4

900g floury potatoes
175ml milk, boiled & strained
5 tablespoons double cream or
  crème fraîche
50g unsalted butter
90g streaky bacon, diced
450g full-fat Tomme, such as
  Cantal, cut into thin slivers
Salt & freshly ground black pepper

Alternative cheeses
Although Cantal is the usual cheese, Gruyère, Emmenthal, fontina and even Lancashire all make good substitutes

Peel the potatoes and cook them in boiling salted water until tender. Drain well and mash until very smooth, then beat in the milk, cream or crème fraîche and butter.

In a separate pan, fry the bacon until it is crisp and the fat has been released. Add the fat (not the bacon itself) to the potato purée and season to taste. Place over a low heat and gradually fold in the cheese using a spatula. Beat the mixture; as it becomes elastic it will soften slightly and eventually be stringy when lifted with the spoon. As soon as it reaches this stage, you should serve the dish immediately.

PG TIPS
Aligot loses its heat fairly quickly, therefore your guests must be ready to eat it at once to appreciate it at its best. Vegetarians may omit the bacon fat.

In my adaptation of this classic Italian dish from Campania, the aubergine slices are rolled up with a cheese, basil and raisin stuffing rather than layered in the usual way. It makes a delicious and substantial vegetarian main course.

involtini di melanzane al **formaggio**

SERVES 4

Olive oil, for frying
2 large aubergines, cut lengthways
 into slices 5mm thick
150ml tomato passata
1 ball of buffalo mozzarella, cut into
 slices 5mm thick
Salt & freshly ground black pepper

For the stuffing
100g provolone, cut into
 small cubes
75g pine kernels
50g raisins, soaked in
 water until plump, then drained
4 tablespoons olive oil
2 tablespoons fresh white
 breadcrumbs
1 garlic clove, crushed
2 tablespoons freshly grated
 Parmesan
1 tablespoon chopped fresh basil
1 egg, beaten

Preheat the oven to 190°C, 375°F, gas 5. Heat a generous quantity of olive oil in a frying pan and fry the aubergine slices a few at a time until golden on both sides, adding more oil if necessary. Drain on kitchen paper and leave to cool.

For the stuffing, mix together the provolone, pine kernels, raisins, olive oil, breadcrumbs, garlic, Parmesan and basil. Season to taste and bind together with the egg. Lay out the cooked aubergine slices on a work surface and divide the stuffing between them. Roll them up fairly tightly to secure the filling and season with salt and pepper. Lightly grease a gratin dish with a little olive oil and put the aubergine rolls in it, packing them in tightly.
Pour over the tomato passata and arrange the mozzarella slices down the centre. Drizzle with a little more olive oil and grind over some salt and pepper, then bake in the oven for 25–30 minutes, until golden. Cool slightly before serving.

PG TIPS
Although this is usually eaten hot, I was once served it cold by an Italian friend whose mother swore that it tasted better cold the next day. You know, I think I have to agree with her. Why not try it, and judge for yourself?

Many people have rosemary bushes growing in their garden but only ever think to put this herb with lamb. Try it in this vegetarian dish and you'll find it partners the courgettes surprisingly well. I suggest you serve the clafoutis as a light main course.

courgette & **cantal** clafoutis with rosemary

SERVES 4

2 tablespoons plain flour
3 eggs
450ml milk
350g courgettes, preferably
  half yellow & half green ones, cut
  into slices 1cm thick
1 garlic clove, crushed
1 tablespoon chopped fresh
  rosemary, plus a few leaves
  to garnish
150g Cantal, thinly sliced
Salt & freshly ground black pepper

Alternative cheese
Cheddar, mild Manchego or
Gorwydd Caerphilly

Preheat the oven to 200°C, 400°F, gas 6. Beat the flour, eggs and milk together to make a smooth batter (or whizz them in a blender). Leave to stand for 20 minutes. Cook the courgettes in boiling salted water for 30 seconds, then drain well and dry them. Arrange them in overlapping circles over the base of a buttered 23cm gratin dish or flan dish and then season with salt and pepper.

Stir the garlic and chopped rosemary into the batter and pour it over the courgettes. Lay the cheese slices on top, scatter over a few rosemary leaves and bake for 30–35 minutes, until golden and well puffed up. Serve warm rather than hot. The clafoutis will sink before serving, so don't be alarmed.

PG TIPS
This recipe makes a good blueprint for all sorts of variations. Try substituting butternut squash for the courgettes, or mushrooms that have been lightly sautéed with garlic, or even a combination of winter squash and mushrooms.

If I am truly honest this dish is only really at its best when the vegetables and cheese can be cooked on an open barbecue over hot coals. Using a pan grill does the job but does not compare in flavour. Not surprisingly, for me, this dish features more often during the hot summer barbecue months.

roasted vegetables with **haloumi** & salsa verde

SERVES 4

4 plum tomatoes, halved
2 medium courgettes, thickly sliced
8 baby leeks, trimmed
12 asparagus tips, peeled
4 tablespoons olive oil
400g haloumi cheese
Salt & freshly ground black pepper

for the salsa verde
40g fresh flat-leaf parsley leaves
2 anchovy fillets
1 teaspoon capers
10 large fresh mint leaves
100ml olive oil

Alternative cheeses
Isle of Mull or mild Parmesan

Preheat the oven to 180°C, 350°F, gas 4. Arrange the vegetables in a baking tin, drizzle over half the olive oil and season. Bake in the oven for 30 minutes or until the vegetables are soft and lightly caramelised. Alternatively, grill on the barbecue.

Cut the haloumi into 1cm thick slices.

Heat the remaining oil in a large non-stick frying pan. When it is hot, add the haloumi slices and cook for 1–2 minutes on each side, until golden brown.

Meanwhile, place all the ingredients for the salsa verde in a small blender and blitz to a course paste.

Arrange the roasted vegetables on 4 serving plates and top with the crisp haloumi. Spoon over the salsa verde and serve.

Every cook has a fantastic recipe for the creamy potato gratin and I'm no exception. Choosing the right waxy potatoes is very important and I always add a little Dijon mustard to the base. Here's the difference: the potatoes are topped with a crumbly Lancashire cheese crust – delicious!

potato gratin with mustard and **lancashire** crumble

SERVES 4

1kg waxy potatoes (Maris Peer, Roseval, Charlotte)
2 garlic cloves, crushed
125g unsalted butter
2 eggs, beaten
300ml double cream
425ml full-fat milk
2 tablespoons Dijon mustard
225g Lancashire cheese, finely grated
1 teaspoon fresh thyme leaves
100g fresh white breadcrumbs
2 tablespoons olive oil
Salt & freshly ground black pepper

Preheat the oven to 190ºC, 375ºF, gas 5. Peel the potatoes, slice them $1/4$cm thick on a kitchen mandolin or with a knife.

Take a large ovenproof dish, rub it lightly with half the garlic and then rub over a little butter. Arrange the potatoes in the dish in overlapping slices, seasoning liberally between each layer. Set aside.

In a bowl, whisk together the eggs, cream, milk and mustard. Pour the mixture over the potatoes and cover them. Dot with the remaining butter.

Place the potatoes in the oven to cook for 50 minutes–1 hour or until the potatoes are tender. (If the potatoes start colouring too much, cover them with tinfoil, by which time most of the cream will have been absorbed.)

In a bowl mix the cheese, thyme and breadcrumbs with the olive oil. Sprinkle the cheese mixture liberally over the potatoes and then return to the oven to bake until golden and crispy in texture.

Allow it to cool slightly before serving directly at your serving table for your guests to tuck in.

These meatless sausages from Wales are also known as Glamorgan sausages and are usually made with Caerphilly or Cheddar cheese and leeks. My favourite version uses Kirkham's Lancashire or sometimes Cornish Yarg. Serve the sausages with a tomato sauce or chutney.

herb cheese sausages

SERVES 4

175g Lancashire or Cornish Yarg, grated
250g fresh white breadcrumbs, plus 100–150g for coating
2 spring onions or small leeks, finely chopped
1 teaspoon mustard powder
1 teaspoon fresh thyme leaves
1 teaspoon chopped fresh rosemary
Freshly grated nutmeg
2 eggs, separated
Flour, for dusting
Vegetable oil, for deep- or shallow-frying
Salt & freshly ground black pepper

Alternative cheeses
Berkswell, Cheddar, Cheshire or Gorwydd Caerphilly

Mix together the cheese, breadcrumbs, spring onions or leeks, mustard and herbs. Season with nutmeg, salt and pepper, then add the egg yolks and knead well to form a soft paste which holds its shape. Chill to firm the mixture up slightly, then shape it into 12 sausages.

Whisk the egg whites just until frothy. Dust the sausages in flour, then dip them in the egg whites and finally roll them in breadcrumbs until thoroughly coated. Deep- or shallow-fry the sausages for 3–4 minutes, or until golden, turning them occasionally. Drain on absorbent paper and serve.

This is more of a 'pudding soufflé' than a heavy pudding. Softer and quicker to ripen than Cheddar, Lancashire is the ultimate toasting cheese. Kirkham's Lancashire is the very best and, although it is usually served only on good cheeseboards, I find it hard to resist using it in cooking too.

lancashire cheese, onion & corn pudding

SERVES 4

50g unsalted butter, plus
   extra for greasing
1 onion, finely chopped
1 large corn on the cob
350ml milk
50g plain flour
1/2 teaspoon mustard
125g Kirkham's Lancashire, grated
Freshly grated nutmeg
4 eggs, separated
Salt & freshly ground black pepper

For the sauce
125ml Vegetable Stock (see page 16)
125g unsalted butter, chilled & diced
2 tomatoes, skinned, deseeded
   & chopped
50g broad beans, cooked
10 fresh basil leaves, shredded

Alternative cheeses
Wensleydale or Gorwydd Caerphilly

Preheat the oven to 180°C, 350°F, gas 4. Heat 25g butter in a heavy-based pan, add the onion, then cover and sweat until tender. Shuck the corn with a knife to remove the kernels. Add them to the onion and sweat for 5 minutes, until soft. Meanwhile, chop the centre husk of the corn into small pieces and place in a pan with the milk. Bring to the boil and simmer for 5 minutes to infuse the milk, then strain.

When the corn and onion are cooked, remove from the pan. Set aside 25g of the corn kernels to use in the sauce. Add the remaining butter to the pan, sprinkle in the flour and stir for 1–2 minutes to form a roux. Pour the infused milk on to the roux a little at a time, blending it in well and stirring constantly to make a thick sauce. Stir in the mustard, cheese, onion and corn and season to taste with nutmeg, salt and pepper. Remove from the heat and cool slightly, then beat in the egg yolks.

Whisk the egg whites until stiff enough to hold their shape. Beat a third of the whites into the corn and cheese mixture, then gently fold in the remaining whites.

Lightly butter four 200ml soufflé dishes and fill them two-thirds full with the mixture. Place in a roasting tin containing enough hot water to come at least halfway up the sides of the dishes. Bake for 20 minutes, until risen and lightly set.

Meanwhile, make the sauce. Bring the stock to the boil in a small pan and boil for 2 minutes. Remove from the heat and whisk in the chilled butter, a few pieces at a time, to form an emulsion. Stir in the tomatoes, broad beans, reserved corn kernels and basil. Season to taste with salt and pepper.

When the puddings are done, cool them slightly before turning them out on to serving plates. Pour the sauce around and serve straight away.

PG TIPS
I find that eggs which are about 1 week old are best for soufflés. I've no idea why! Don't allow the cheese and corn mixture to become completely cold before adding the beaten egg whites, or the puddings will not rise to their full extent.

A simple but great-tasting vegetable dish to serve with meat or fish, or even as a breakfast accompaniment. Try the potato cakes for brunch, topped with a poached egg and Hollandaise sauce as a variation on eggs Benedict.

potato cakes with **ricotta** & chives

SERVES 4

675g potatoes
50g unsalted butter
2 shallots, finely chopped
75g plain flour
1 egg
1 egg yolk
75g firm ricotta
2 tablespoons chopped fresh chives
Freshly grated nutmeg
3 tablespoons clarified butter
  (see Tip on page 83) or
  vegetable oil
Salt & freshly ground black pepper

Alternative cheeses
Fresh goat's cheese or a grated
hard cheese

Cook the potatoes in their skins in simmering salted water until tender, then drain well. Peel and sieve while still hot; you will need 450g sieved potato. Heat the butter in a pan, add the shallots and sweat until tender but not coloured. Stir in the flour to make a thick roux and cook for 1 minute over a low heat. Remove from the heat, beat in the egg and egg yolk and then beat in the sieved potato, ricotta and chives. Season with nutmeg, salt and pepper and then leave to cool.

Shape the mixture into 8 potato cakes and fry in the clarified butter or oil for 4–5 minutes on each side, until golden. Serve immediately.

PG TIPS
You can use the potato cake mixture to make delicious gnocchi by rolling it into small balls and poaching them in boiling salted water. Put them in a gratin dish, pour a richly flavoured tomato sauce on top, and sprinkle them with grated Parmesan or Cheddar. Then brown the gnocchi under the grill.

This potato and cheese mash is particularly good served with roast or grilled chicken or lamb.

goat's cheese & parsley mash

SERVES 4

750g potatoes, peeled & cut
  into chunks
250ml milk, warmed
50g softened unsalted butter
100g soft goat's cheese
  such as Roubiliac, sieved
2 tablespoons chopped fresh
  flat-leaf parsley
Freshly grated nutmeg
Salt & freshly ground black pepper

Put the potatoes in a pan of cold salted water and bring to the boil, then simmer until tender. Drain the potatoes and, while still hot, sieve them or mash well.

Beat in the warm milk and the butter, then fold in the sieved goat's cheese and parsley. Season with nutmeg, salt and pepper and serve immediately.

PG TIPS

When it comes to preparing potato mash of any kind, I believe there is no better potato than the Desirée, with its superb dry texture and good flavour. It is well worth making the effort to find this variety.

Swede is still too reminiscent of school dinners for many people's tastes yet in the right hands it can be one of the most flavourful vegetables. Potato mashes are currently very fashionable but perhaps swede mash is the one to watch for the future! This recipe is also good when made with parsnips.

swede mash with cheddar & black pepper butter

SERVES 4

675g swede, peeled & cut
  into small cubes
2 tablespoons olive oil
4 tablespoons milk
100g mild Cheddar, grated
65g unsalted butter
1 teaspoon cracked black pepper
  (see Tip)
Salt

Cook the swede in boiling salted water until tender, then drain well. Purée in a blender with the oil and milk until smooth. Transfer to a clean pan and heat through, then beat in the Cheddar and 15g of the butter. Season with salt to taste, then transfer to a warmed serving dish.

Melt the remaining butter with the cracked black pepper, pour it over the purée and serve straight away.

PG TIPS

To make cracked black pepper, put some peppercorns in a small bowl and break them up roughly with the end of a rolling pin, or use a pestle and mortar.

chapter 7 **cold desserts & warm puddings**

Sambuca is an Italian anisette liqueur. If you don't have any, you could use a fruit brandy or ordinary brandy instead. This easy dessert makes a great finale to a barbecue.

sambuca-flamed **ricotta** with chilled summer berries

SERVES 4

250g firm ricotta
50g caster sugar, or to taste
125ml Sambuca
100ml double cream, semi-whipped
200g mixed berries,
  such as raspberries, strawberries
  & redcurrants, chilled
75g white chocolate, cut
  into shavings (optional)

Beat the ricotta, sugar and 3 tablespoons of the Sambuca together until creamy. Gently fold in the double cream and transfer to a serving bowl. Chill for at least 4 hours.

Just before serving, heat the remaining Sambuca in a small pan until very hot and pour it over the ricotta mixture. Ignite with a match; then, when the flames have died down, top with the chilled summer berries. Scatter over the white chocolate shavings, if using, and serve immediately.

PG TIPS
Try serving this with a fresh berry coulis on the side. The addition of a few toasted, flaked almonds and a little sprig of mint makes an attractive decoration and alternative to the chocolate shavings.

For an interesting contrast, you could serve the rhubarb and punch syrup with the sorbet while they are still warm.

rhubarb in chilled punch syrup with **cheese** sorbet

SERVES 4

350ml red wine
4 tablespoons grenadine syrup
Juice & zest of 1 orange
1 cinnamon stick
75g caster sugar
750g rhubarb, peeled &
 cut into 5cm lengths

For the cheese sorbet
500ml milk
175g caster sugar
Juice & zest of 1 small orange
175g cream cheese

For the sorbet, put the milk, sugar, orange juice and zest in a pan and bring to the boil, stirring to dissolve the sugar, then remove from the heat and leave to cool. Stir this mixture into the cream cheese. Pour into an ice-cream maker and freeze until firm, following the manufacturer's instructions.

If you don't have an ice-cream maker, pour the mixture into a shallow container and put it in the freezer. After about 30 minutes, when the mixture is beginning to set, remove from the freezer and beat well with an electric beater or hand whisk to disperse any ice crystals, then return it to the freezer. Repeat this 2 or 3 times and then freeze until firm.

For the punch syrup, put the wine, grenadine syrup, orange juice and zest, cinnamon and sugar into a pan and boil until reduced by half its volume. Add the rhubarb to the syrup and cook gently for up to 5 minutes, until the rhubarb is tender and sweet but still holds its shape. Transfer to a bowl and leave to cool, then chill thoroughly. Serve with scoops of the cheese sorbet.

I first prepared this unusual dessert to an influential group of food press with great aplomb! On that occasion, apples were used instead of pears in the filling but either are delicious. I particularly like to serve this charlotte with a good dollop of clotted cream.

pear, **jarlsberg** & date charlotte

SERVES 6

450g stale bread
 (approx 12–15 slices)
Softened unsalted butter

for the filling
375g pears
50g unsalted butter
50g caster sugar
2 tablespoons soaked raisins
75g stoned dates, cut into pieces
2 tablespoons chopped walnuts
50g Jarlsberg cheese, grated

for the apricot sauce
250g peeled fresh apricots or tinned
 in their syrup
2 tablespoons apricot brandy
Juice of 1/2 lime

to serve
Clotted cream or pouring cream
 and a little icing sugar to dust
 the charlottes

Alternative cheeses
Wensleydale

Preheat the oven to 220ºC, 425ºF, gas 7. Cut 12 slices of the bread into discs, to fit the bases of 6 large metal pudding or dariole moulds, as well as 6 to fit the tops. Cut away the crusts of the remaining slices of bread and cut into 2 1/2 cm fingers. Butter all the bread on one side only. Place a disc butter-side down in the base of each mould. The fingers can now easily be laid, butter-side against the mould, slightly over-lapping all the way around. Place to one side.

For the filling, peel the pears, remove the centre cores and cut into 1cm chunks. Melt half the butter in a pan and, when hot, add the pear and cook for 1 minute before adding the sugar. Continue cooking for a further few minutes until the pears are golden. Add the raisins, dates and walnuts and mix well. Remove from the heat and stir in the Jarlsberg.

Divide the mixture between the 6 lined charlottes and then top with the lids. Any excess bread at the sides can be folded over, to keep the lids in place. Bake in the oven for 20–25 minutes, until golden and crisp.

Meanwhile, prepare a quick apricot sauce by pureéing the apricots and their syrup in a blender. Add the apricot brandy and lime juice and mix well.

Once the charlottes are cooked, remove them from the oven and leave to rest for 2–3 minutes, then turn out the charlottes onto plates. Dust lightly with icing sugar. Garnish with the clotted cream and serve with the apricot sauce.

You may be surprised by this combination of caramelised apples, sweet blackberries and savoury camembert cheese. But, prepared in the style of a classic brulée, the flavours work really well together and make a sensational dessert. Be sure to serve with lashings of double cream.

toffee apple **camembert** & blackberry pudding

SERVES 8

25g unsalted butter
6 tablespoons caster sugar
4 granny smith apples, peeled,
  cored and diced
60ml calvados apple brandy
250ml full-fat milk
500ml whipping cream
125g Coeur De Lion Camembert
  cheese, cut into small dice
6 egg yolks
1 teaspoon vanilla extract
100g quince jelly
8 slices brioche (or white bread)
300g blackberries
Icing sugar to dust

Preheat the oven to 150ºC, 300ºF, gas 2. Heat the butter in a non-stick frying pan over a low heat, add the diced apple and half of the sugar and cook for 10–12 minutes, until the apple is caramelised. Flambé with the brandy and set aside to cool.

Put the milk and three quarters of the caramelised apple in a blender and blitz until smooth. In a pan, simmer the cream with the apple mixture, add the diced camembert and allow to dissolve, but do not boil.

In a bowl, combine the egg yolk, remaining sugar and vanilla extract. Mix well until light and fluffy. Pour the cream mixture into the yolks whilst stirring constantly, and then strain through a fine strainer.

Melt the quince jelly with 3 tablespoons of water in a pan until dissolved. Cut the brioche slices in half diagonally and then brush both sides with the quince mixture. Layer the bread, the remaining caramelised apples and the blackberries neatly in a shallow ovenproof dish. Pour over the apple cheese cream.

Place the dish in a large baking dish. Add enough boiling water to come halfway up the sides of the dish. Place the pudding in the oven, uncovered, for about 40–45 minutes until the cream cheese has just set and the pudding is lightly brown.

Dust with a little icing sugar and glaze before serving.

PG TIPS
Serve with a little pouring cream or cider apple sorbet. Figs make a lovely alternative to the blackberries in the dish.

You may be surprised to see goat's cheese in an ice-cream but it gives it a delicious tanginess. The ice-cream makes a wonderful foil for cherries – try it with a warm cherry tart or clafoutis. I have included instructions for freezing without an ice-cream maker, though I believe that for fine-textured ice-creams and sorbets you do need to invest in a machine. They are quite reasonably priced now and once you have one the possibilities are endless.

goat's cheese ice-cream

SERVES 8

500ml milk
125ml double cream
4 egg yolks
1 egg
90g caster sugar
125g mild soft goat's cheese, such
  as Sainte-Maure or
  mild Ribblesdale

Bring the milk and double cream to the boil. Whisk the egg yolks, whole egg and sugar together until thick, pale and creamy. Pour the milk and cream slowly on to the eggs, whisking all the time. Return the mixture to the pan and stir with a wooden spoon over a gentle heat until it has thickened enough to coat the back of the spoon. Do not let it boil or the eggs will scramble. Remove from the heat and stir in the cheese until it has melted into the custard. Pass through a fine sieve and leave to cool.

Pour the mixture into an ice-cream maker and freeze according to the manufacturer's instructions. If you don't have an ice-cream maker, pour the ice-cream into a shallow container and place it in the freezer. After about 30 minutes, when it is beginning to set, remove it from the freezer and beat with an electric beater or hand whisk to disperse any ice crystals, then return it to the freezer. Repeat 2 or 3 times and then freeze until firm.

This is a shamelessly indulgent confection, rich and sticky and quite irresistible. Make sure you buy the very best quality dates, such as the succulent Medjool variety, in order to do it justice.

brie ice-cream with dates, walnuts & butterscotch sauce

SERVES 8

Ingredients for the Goat's Cheese
  Ice-cream (above), replacing the
  goat's cheese with 125g semi-
  ripe Brie
150g dates, stoned & cut into strips
2 tablespoons walnuts, in large
  pieces

For the butterscotch sauce
75g soft brown sugar
90ml double cream
75g unsalted butter
1/2 teaspoon vanilla extract

Remove the rind from the Brie and cut the cheese into small pieces. Make the ice-cream as for the Goat's Cheese Ice-cream and freeze until firm.

For the sauce, put all the ingredients in a heavy-based saucepan and cook over a medium heat for 3–5 minutes, stirring all the time, until the colour changes to a light caramel. Leave to cool and then chill.

To serve, put scoops of ice-cream in glass coupes and scatter over the dates and walnuts. Lightly coat with the chilled butterscotch sauce.

Panna cotta, meaning cooked cream, is a traditional Piedmontese pudding of moulded cream lightly set with gelatine. Unconventionally, this recipe includes ricotta, so I have christened it Panna 'Ri-cotta'. Moving even further away from tradition, it is flavoured with coffee and served with a fresh apricot compote.

panna 'ri-cotta'

SERVES 4

4 tablespoons milk
150ml double cream
75g caster sugar
Zest of 1/2 orange
100ml freshly made strong coffee,
 preferably espresso
1/2 vanilla pod, split
2 gelatine leaves
2 tablespoons rum
200g firm ricotta, sieved
Sprigs of fresh mint, to decorate
 (optional)

For the apricot compote
75g caster sugar
90ml water
Juice of 1/2 lemon
350g fresh apricots, stoned & sliced

Put the milk, cream, sugar and orange zest in a pan and bring to the boil. Stir in the coffee and scrape in the seeds from the vanilla pod, then add the pod as well. Remove from the heat and leave to cool. Meanwhile, put the gelatine in a small pan, cover with cold water and leave to soak for 5 minutes. Heat gently until the gelatine has dissolved.

Take the vanilla pod out of the pan and stir in the rum, sieved ricotta and the gelatine. Strain through a fine sieve, then pour into 4 ramekins or similar moulds and chill for at least 2 hours, until set.

For the compote, put the sugar, water and lemon juice in a pan and bring slowly to the boil, stirring to dissolve the sugar. Reduce the heat, add the sliced apricots and poach for about 5 minutes, until just tender. Remove from the heat and leave to cool, then chill.

Turn out the coffee ricotta custards, or serve them in the ramekins if you prefer, accompanied by the apricot compote and decorated with sprigs of mint, if liked.

In this sumptuous dessert, crushed caramelised nuts are folded into a quark and whipped cream mixture which is used to fill meringue shells. The pavlovas are then decorated with candied pineapple rings. The recipe looks quite complicated, but all the separate components can be prepared well in advance and then put together shortly before serving.

crunchy **quark** pavlovas with caramelised pineapple

SERVES 6

4 egg whites
225g caster sugar
1 teaspoon vinegar
200g quark
200ml double cream

For the florentine
75g caster sugar
75g hazelnuts, chopped
75g flaked almonds

For the carmelised pineapple
100g caster sugar
200ml water
1 small, ripe pineapple, peeled,
  cored & thinly sliced into rings

The pavlovas can be prepared a day in advance. Preheat the oven to 110°C, 225°F, gas ¼. Whisk the egg whites until they form stiff peaks and then gradually whisk in two-thirds of the caster sugar and the vinegar. Fold in the rest of the caster sugar by hand. Take 6 metal rings, 7.5cm in diameter, place them on a baking sheet and fill with the meringue (alternatively pipe it into circles on baking parchment). Carefully remove the rings and bake the meringues for 1–1½ hours, until crisp on the outside. Leave in the turned-off oven to cool.

For the florentine, put the sugar in a heavy-based pan and melt over a medium heat, then raise the heat and cook until it is a deep golden brown. Stir in the nuts with a wooden spoon, pour the mixture on to a lightly oiled baking tray, spreading it evenly, and leave to go hard. Place the nut caramel in a small plastic bag and crush to large crumbs with the end of a rolling pin – or use a food processor.

For the caramelised pineapple, bring the sugar and water to the boil. Add the pineapple rings, reduce the heat and cook gently for about 30–45 minutes, until the pineapple becomes translucent. Leave to cool in the syrup.

Whisk the quark and cream together until thick, then fold in the crushed florentine, retaining 50g to decorate the pavlovas.

To serve, turn the meringues over and carefully scoop out the centre from the base of each one, leaving a thin shell. Fill them with the quark cream and turn right-side up again. Place on individual serving plates and decorate with the slices of pineapple. Drizzle over the pineapple syrup and sprinkle over the remaining florentine.

This looks like a classic crème brûlée, but when you shatter the crisp caramel topping a thin layer of dark chocolate is revealed underneath. You could put a handful of raspberries at the bottom of each dish for another unexpected treat.

chocolate **mascarpone** brûlée

SERVES 4

425g mascarpone
175g caster sugar
6 egg yolks
50g good-quality plain chocolate
Icing sugar, for dusting

Preheat the oven to 140°C, 275°F, gas 1. Lightly whisk together the cheese, two-thirds of the caster sugar and all the egg yolks and then strain through a sieve. Pour the mixture into 4 ramekins and place them on a wad of paper in a roasting tin (the paper prevents the mixture at the bottom of the dishes getting too hot). Pour boiling water into the roasting tin to come halfway up the sides of each dish and bake for 30–35 minutes, or until the custards are just firm to the touch. Remove from the oven, take the dishes out of the roasting tin and leave to cool, then chill thoroughly.

Melt the chocolate and spread it evenly over each mascarpone custard. Return them to the refrigerator for 15 minutes so the chocolate sets hard, then sprinkle the remaining caster sugar over the top. Place under a preheated very hot grill until the sugar is golden and bubbling, then leave to cool. Dust the edges with a little icing sugar before serving.

PG TIPS
A very effective method is to use a small domestic blowtorch to glaze the brûlées instead of putting them under the grill.

Purple figs are best for this dish. During summer I like to serve some fresh berries sprinkled around the figs.

poached figs stuffed with **sainte-maure** cheese in merlot wine syrup

SERVES 4

16 ripe but firm figs
100g Sainte-Maure goat's cheese
50g mascarpone
Zest of 1 lemon
2 tablespoons caster sugar

For the syrup
100g caster sugar
1 bottle of Merlot (or other red wine)
1 cinnamon stick

Alternative cheeses
Any soft goat's cheese such as mild Ribblesdale or Montrachet (US). The Australian Kervella goat ricotta makes an interesting alternative

For the syrup, put the sugar, wine and cinnamon in a saucepan that is just large enough to hold the figs in a single layer. Bring slowly to the boil, stirring to dissolve the sugar, and simmer for 4–5 minutes. Add the figs and poach for 4–5 minutes, or until just tender. Remove the figs with a slotted spoon. Boil the syrup until reduced to half its volume.

Purée 4 of the figs in a blender, adding enough of the reduced poaching syrup to give a sauce-like consistency. Strain and chill.

Beat together the Sainte-Maure, mascarpone, lemon zest and sugar. Slice the tops off the 12 remaining figs, fill with the cheese mixture and replace the tops. Arrange the figs on 4 serving plates, pour the sauce around and serve.

The caramel offsets the sharpness of the yogurt cheese, resulting in a simple dessert with complex flavours. This is really quite a straightforward recipe but you need to start preparations 3–4 days in advance, in order to drain the yogurt for the labna.

pepper-caramel roasted pears with **labna**

SERVES 4

250g live Greek yogurt
1/2 teaspoon ground cinnamon
125g soft brown sugar
175ml water
1 cinnamon stick, broken into
  3 pieces
1/4 teaspoon cracked black pepper
  (see Tip on page 146)
4 ripe but firm Williams pears
50g unsalted butter
90ml Poire William or brandy

Alternative cheeses
A blue cheese like Dolcelatte Torta or curd cheese also goes well with the pears

Mix the Greek yogurt with the ground cinnamon and then drain it through muslin for 3–4 days, as described in the recipe for Labna on page 185.

Preheat the oven to 180°C, 350°F, gas 4. Put the sugar in a heavy-based saucepan and leave over a low heat until melted. Raise the heat until it has caramelised lightly, then carefully pour in the water (the syrup may splutter) and add the cinnamon stick and cracked black pepper. Boil for 10–12 minutes to form a light syrup.

Peel the pears carefully so as to keep their shape, then cut them in half, leaving the stalks intact. Remove the cores.

Heat the butter in a large, shallow, flameproof casserole or an ovenproof frying pan, add the pear halves, flat-side down, and cook until lightly coloured. Pour over the Poire William or brandy, turn the pears over, then pour over the syrup. Transfer to the oven and bake for 40 minutes, basting the pears with the syrup once or twice to form a light glaze. Remove from the oven and cool to room temperature. To serve, top each pear half with a scoop of the labna.

Try to get really good prunes for this, preferably French Agen prunes or the large, moist Californian variety. I like to serve the tart with a fresh orange sauce, such as the one with My Favourite Pick-me-up on page 152.

quark, prune & white chocolate tart

SERVES 4–6

½ quantity of sweet pastry
 (see page 21)
100g white chocolate
2 gelatine leaves
4 tablespoons dry white wine
Juice & zest of 1 orange
4 egg yolks
25g caster sugar
125g quark
150ml double cream, semi-whipped
10 prunes, soaked overnight in
 4 tablespoons Armagnac or brandy

Alternative cheese
Any curd cheese

Preheat the oven to 190°C, 375°F, gas 5. Roll out the pastry and use to line a 20cm tart tin. Line with greaseproof paper, fill with baking beans and bake blind for 8–10 minutes. Remove the paper and beans and bake for a further 5 minutes, then take out of the oven and leave to cool.

Melt the white chocolate in a small bowl set over a pan of hot water. Brush the base of the cooled pastry case with about two-thirds of the melted chocolate and set aside.

Cover the gelatine leaves with a little water and leave to soak for 5 minutes. Bring the wine, orange juice and zest to the boil in a pan. Whisk together the egg yolks and sugar in a bowl for 2–3 minutes, until creamy. Gradually pour the wine and orange mixture on to the yolks, whisking all the time. Cool slightly, then add the soaked and drained gelatine leaves and stir until dissolved. Fold in the remaining melted chocolate.

When the mixture is almost cold and just beginning to set, gently but thoroughly fold in the quark and the semi-whipped cream. Arrange the prunes in the pastry case, then pour in the filling. Chill for at least 2 hours for it to set.

PG TIPS
Don't serve the tart too cold, as this impairs the flavour. Remove it from the refrigerator and bring it to room temperature about 15 minutes before serving.

I devised this recipe for the Christmas edition of the BBC Vegetarian Good Food magazine, when looking for an alternative to the traditional Christmas plum pudding.

dried fruit & **mascarpone** fool with saffron & ginger syrup

SERVES 6–8

450g dried apricots
600ml water
100g mixed dried fruit, such as
   apricots, prunes & figs, cut
   into large pieces
100g caster sugar
Juice & zest of 1 lemon
6 tablespoons apricot brandy (or
   orange liqueur such as cointreau
   or Grand Marnier)
300ml double cream
100g mascarpone
Sprigs of fresh mint, to decorate
   (optional)

For the saffron & ginger syrup
2 tablespoons syrup from a jar of
   stem ginger
Juice & zest of 1 orange
200ml water
A good pinch of saffron strands

Put the dried apricots in a saucepan, pour the water over and leave to soak overnight. Bring all the ingredients for the saffron and ginger syrup to the boil, pour it over the mixed dried fruit and leave that to soak overnight too.

The next day, bring the dried apricots to the boil, then reduce the heat and simmer for 20–25 minutes until soft, adding a little more water if necessary. Transfer to a blender with the sugar, lemon juice and zest and apricot brandy and blitz to a smooth purée. Leave to cool.

Whip the cream until it is just beginning to thicken. Beat the mascarpone just to soften it and then fold it gently into the cream. Fold two-thirds of the apricot purée into this mixture. Pour the fool into tall glasses until they are almost half full. Put a spoonful of the apricot purée on top and then top up with more fool, until the mixture is 2cm below the rim of the glasses. Chill for 4 hours.

To serve, top up the glasses with the mixed dried fruit in syrup and decorate with the mint sprigs, if using.

No book on cheese cookery would be complete without a recipe for cheesecake. I prefer the uncooked variety, so here is one of my favourites that I make at home, using autumn produce. If you can't get wild loganberries, try blackberries, blueberries or raspberries, or a mixture.

wild loganberry & roasted hazelnut **cheesecake**

2 eggs, separated
75g caster sugar
225g wild loganberries,
  plus a few extra to decorate
2 gelatine leaves
350g full-fat cream cheese
150ml double cream, semi-whipped

For the base
100g digestive biscuits
25g demerara sugar
25g hazelnuts, roasted
  (see Tip on page 73), skinned
  & chopped
50g unsalted butter, melted

For the sauce
225g wild loganberries
Juice of 1 lemon, or to taste
Caster sugar, to taste

For the base, put the digestive biscuits in a food processor and blitz until they resemble coarse breadcrumbs. Transfer to a bowl and stir in the demerara sugar, chopped hazelnuts and melted butter. The mixture should be sticky but not wet. Press it firmly over the base of a 20cm springform cake tin.

Put the egg yolks and sugar in a bowl set over a pan of simmering water, making sure the water is not touching the base of the bowl. Whisk with a hand-held electric beater until the mixture is thick and creamy in colour; the beaters should leave a trail on the surface when lifted. Remove the bowl from the pan of water and leave to cool, whisking occasionally.

Purée the loganberries in a blender and then push through a fine sieve. Put the gelatine in a pan with 3 tablespoons water and leave for 5 minutes, then place over a very low heat until dissolved and clear. Mix the puréed loganberries with the egg yolk mixture, then stir in the melted gelatine. Add the cream cheese and mix in thoroughly. Whisk the egg whites until stiff and fold them in. Finally, fold in the whipped cream. Pour the mixture into the cake tin and smooth the top with a palette knife. Chill for at least 2 hours, until set.

Meanwhile, make the sauce. Put the loganberries in a blender with the lemon juice and a little sugar and blitz until smooth. Pass through a fine sieve and add a little more lemon juice or sugar to taste, if necessary. Serve the cheesecake with the sauce, decorated with a few extra loganberries, if liked.

Here, the famous crémet d'Anjou mixture of cream and soft cheese is blended with a tart blackberry purée and served sandwiched between caramelised pastry wafers. It is quite some combination.

caramelised pastry wafers with blackberry **crémet**

SERVES 4

200g cream cheese or fromage frais
200ml double cream or crème
  fraîche, semi-whipped
2 egg whites
25g caster sugar
100g puff pastry
75g icing sugar

For the blackberry purée
250g fresh blackberries
75g caster sugar
A little lemon juice

Put the cream cheese or fromage frais in a bowl and beat until smooth, then fold in the whipped cream or crème fraîche. Whisk the egg whites until they form stiff peaks. Fold in the caster sugar and then fold the egg whites into the cream cheese mixture. Set aside.

Put 100g of the blackberries in a blender, add the sugar and blitz to a purée. Transfer to a bowl and balance the sweetness with a squeeze of lemon juice. Add half the purée to the cheese mixture and gently fold it through to give a marbled effect. Cover and place in the refrigerator for about 12 hours, preferably overnight.

Preheat the oven to 220°C, 425°F, gas 7. For the pastry wafers, roll out the puff pastry in a rectangle about 15 x 25cm and approximately 2mm thick. Dust with a little of the icing sugar, then roll it up very tightly like a Swiss roll. Place in a very cold refrigerator or a freezer for a short while to firm up, then with a sharp knife cut the roll into 12 slices about 5mm thick. (You won't need all the pastry but you can freeze the rest for later use.) Liberally dust the slices with the remaining icing sugar and roll them out as thinly as possible into ovals. Place them on a baking sheet and bake for 8–10 minutes, or until golden and caramelised. Remove from the oven and place on a wire rack to cool.

To serve, put a wafer on each of 4 serving plates and cover with some of the marbled cheese mixture. Place another wafer on top, cover with more cheese mixture, then top with a final wafer. Stir the remaining blackberries into the remaining purée and arrange around the wafer stacks.

PG TIPS
Pipe the cheese mixture over the pastry wafers for a professional finish. These crisp pastry wafers are also good as an accompaniment to ice-cream or sorbet. They keep for up to a week in a sealed container in a dry, cool place.

I love the refreshing taste of these summer berries, offset with a sweet cheese sauce. Other fruit such as apricots or peaches can be used, or even poached pears during the colder months. Why not try serving the apricot Stilton sauce as a fondue for dipping fruits? In this case, a little apricot brandy may be added instead of kirsch.

summer fruit gratin with apricot **stilton** sauce

SERVES 4

250g fresh blackberries
50g caster sugar, or to taste
450g mixed fresh
  summer berries, such as
  strawberries, blackberries,
  raspberries, redcurrants

For the sauce
90ml double cream
75g white apricot Stilton, grated
2 egg yolks
50g caster sugar
Kirsch, to taste

Alternative cheeses
Any cream cheese could be
substituted for the Stilton

Place the blackberries in a blender with the sugar and blitz to a purée. Strain the purée through a fine sieve to remove the pips. Taste and add more sugar if necessary.

For the sauce, bring the cream to the boil in a pan, then remove from the heat and stir in the cheese. Leave to cool. Put the egg yolks and sugar in a bowl set over a pan of simmering water, making sure the water does not touch the base of the bowl. Whisk until the mixture becomes pale and thick and doubles in volume. Remove the bowl from the heat and continue to whisk until the mixture is cold. Fold in the cheese and cream mixture and then add kirsch to taste.

Toss the mixed berries with the blackberry purée and pile them up in the centre of 4 heatproof serving plates. Carefully pour the cheese sauce around the fruit and put the plates under a hot grill to glaze the cheese sauce until light golden in colour.
Serve immediately.

A simple, light, lemon-scented pancake topped with ricotta and fresh raspberries and served with raspberry sauce. I like it for dessert with a scoop of vanilla ice-cream, but it also makes an excellent brunch dish. For a winter version you could fill the blini with poached pears instead of raspberries. To make chocolate blini, replace 2 tablespoons of the flour with cocoa powder.

lemon blini with **ricotta** & raspberries

SERVES 4

20g caster sugar
Finely grated zest of 1 lemon
100g self-raising flour
1/2 teaspoon baking powder
2 teaspoons melted butter
150ml milk
2 eggs, separated
A pinch each of salt & sugar
1 tablespoon olive oil
4 tablespoons ricotta, drained
200g fresh raspberries
Icing sugar, for dusting
Sprigs of fresh mint, to decorate
  (optional)

For the sauce
250g fresh raspberries
Juice of 1/2 lemon, or to taste
75g icing sugar, or to taste

Alternative cheese
Quark, Marscapone or
Brillat Savarin

For the blini, mix together the sugar and lemon zest to extract the lemon's natural oils. Sift the flour and baking powder into a bowl and stir in the sugar mixture. In a separate bowl, whisk together the melted butter, milk and egg yolks, then combine with the flour to make a batter. Whisk the egg whites with a pinch of salt and sugar until they form stiff peaks, then fold them into the batter. Leave to stand for 5–10 minutes.

Meanwhile, make the sauce. Purée the raspberries in a blender, then pass them through a fine sieve. Stir in the lemon juice and icing sugar, adjusting the quantities to taste if necessary.

To cook the blini, heat the olive oil in a heavy-based frying pan over a gentle heat (or individual blini pans if you happen to have them). Then drop in 2 tablespoons of batter for each pancake so that they are about 10cm in diameter. Cook for about 2 minutes, until bubbles start to appear on the surface, then flip them over and cook the other side. Keep them warm while you cook the remaining blini – you need 8 in all.

Carefully spread the ricotta over 4 of the blini, then cover with the raspberries. Top with the other 4 blini and put on serving plates. Dust with icing sugar, pour the raspberry sauce around and serve, decorated with sprigs of mint if liked.

PG TIPS
I've found that American pancake and waffle mixes make a good alternative to the flour and baking powder, producing soft, light pancakes.

Corsican food is typically Mediterranean but has a few distinctive hallmarks, one of which is the use of Broccio, a sheep's milk cheese. Broccio is popular in savoury dishes and desserts such as fritters, custards and this simple omelette. It's quite hard to obtain elsewhere, so I have substituted goat's cheese, which I actually prefer.

corsican-style **goat's cheese** & honey omelette

SERVES 4

6 eggs, beaten
1 tablespoon chopped fresh mint
65g caster sugar
65g ground almonds

50g unsalted butter
75g soft goat's cheese,
  such as Roubiliac, thinly sliced
2 tablespoons clear honey
Icing sugar, for dusting

Put the eggs in a bowl with the mint, sugar, ground almonds and 1 tablespoon cold water and beat until light and fluffy. Heat the butter in a 20cm omelette pan. When it is foaming, pour in the beaten eggs and stir with a fork. When half set, arrange the goat's cheese slices over the top. Allow to soften slightly, then spoon over the honey and fold the omelette – or leave it flat, if you prefer. Dust with icing sugar and serve warm.

Wensleydale cheese should be eaten young and fresh and is delicious with crisp autumn fruits such as apples and pears. This pie is one of my favourite old English puddings, a traditional Yorkshire way of combining apples and cheese. In this recipe the cheese is mixed with the apples for the filling, but often it is included in the pastry instead. Another Yorkshire custom is to serve a good wedge of crumbly Wensleydale with a slice of rich fruit cake or a mince pie.

spiced apple & **wensleydale** pie

SERVES 4

500g cooking apples, peeled, cored
  & chopped
A pinch of ground cloves
1 teaspoon ground cinnamon
A pinch of freshly grated nutmeg
50g raisins
75g caster sugar
75g Wensleydale cheese,
  broken into small chunks
1/2 quantity of shortcrust pastry
  (see page 21)
1 egg beaten with 1 tablespoon
  water, to glaze

Preheat the oven to 200°C, 400°F, gas 6. Mix together the apples, spices, raisins, sugar and cheese and place in a deep 20cm pie dish. Roll out the pastry a little larger than the pie dish. Cut a thin strip from around the edge and press it on to the rim of the dish, then brush with a little of the beaten egg. Cover the pie with the pastry, pressing it on to the rim and trimming the edges. Flute the edges neatly and make a hole in the centre.

Roll out the pastry trimmings and cut out leaves or whatever shape you like. Use to decorate the pie. Brush all over with the beaten egg and bake for 15–20 minutes, until the pastry is golden. Reduce the oven temperature to 160°C, 325°F, gas 3 and bake for a further 25 minutes. Serve hot or warm, with a light custard sauce or thick clotted cream.

When we were creating recipes for this book, my sous-chefs and I came across many remarkable combinations that pleasantly surprised us. None more so than this recipe pairing prune soufflé with goat's cheese ice-cream, which has turned out to be one of my favourites. Try it, and I think you'll see why.

hot prune soufflé with **goat's cheese** ice-cream

SERVES 4

75g pitted prunes,
  preferably Agen prunes
40g unsalted butter, plus extra
  for greasing
40g plain flour
200ml milk, boiled & strained
5 eggs, separated
2 tablespoons Armagnac
75g caster sugar,
  plus extra for dusting
15g cornflour
4 scoops of Goat's Cheese Ice-cream
  (see page 154)

Lightly butter 4 soufflé dishes, 200ml in capacity, and then dust with a little sugar, shaking out any excess. Preheat the oven to 200°C, 400°F, gas 6.

Simmer the prunes in water to cover until soft. Purée them in a blender and set aside. Melt the butter in a saucepan, stir in the flour and cook for 1–2 minutes. Gradually stir in the milk to form a thick sauce and simmer for 5 minutes. Stir in the prune purée, remove from the heat and leave to cool. Beat in the egg yolks and Armagnac.

Whisk the egg whites until they form stiff peaks, then gradually whisk in the sugar. Finally, whisk in the cornflour. Beat a third of the egg whites into the prune sauce and then gently fold in the rest. Pour the mixture into the soufflé dishes and put them in a roasting tin containing enough water to come two-thirds of the way up the sides of the dishes. Bake in the oven for 15–20 minutes, until well risen. Serve immediately, with the ice-cream on the side.

PG TIPS
A nice touch is to break open the soufflés at the table and put a scoop of the goat's cheese ice-cream in the centre of each one. You could also make extra prune purée and drizzle it over the ice-cream.

Another variation on the cheese and apple pie theme (see Spiced Apple and Wensleydale Pie on page 172), this time with an Italian flavour. A simple dollop of fresh cream is all you need to accompany it, but if you prefer something a little more elaborate, try a compote of plums or prunes. Strudel pastry can be time-consuming to make, but filo is generally accepted as a convenient substitute nowadays.

apple **pecorino** strudel

SERVES 6–8

50g fresh white breadcrumbs
50g ground almonds
100g unsalted butter
900g cooking apples,
  peeled, cored & thinly sliced
50g caster sugar
1 teaspoon ground cinnamon
1/2 teaspoon ground mixed spice
50g raisins, soaked in water
  until plump
25g walnuts or almonds, chopped
Zest of 1/2 lemon
150g pecorino Romano, thinly sliced
4 large sheets of filo pastry, about
  45 x 30cm
Icing sugar, for dusting

Alternative cheese
Ricotta makes a tasty alternative
to the pecorino or similar firmer
cheeses like Jarlsberg

Preheat the oven to 200°C, 400°F, gas 6. Fry the breadcrumbs and ground almonds in 50g of the butter until lightly golden, then set aside.

Mix together the apples, sugar, cinnamon, mixed spice, raisins, nuts and lemon zest. Carefully fold in the pecorino cheese.

Melt the remaining butter. Lay out 1 sheet of filo dough on a work surface and brush with some of the butter, then top with the remaining sheets of filo, brushing with butter between the layers. Brush the final sheet of pastry with more butter and sprinkle the fried breadcrumb mixture over the top. Spread the apple mixture over the surface and roll up the pastry to form a compact roll. Transfer to a greased baking sheet, curving the strudel to fit if necessary, and brush with the remaining melted butter. Bake for 20–25 minutes, until crisp and golden.

Remove from the oven, dust generously with icing sugar and serve hot.

PG TIPS
If your filo pastry is smaller than the size given in the recipe, use extra sheets and lay them out on the work surface, overlapping the edges, to form a rectangle about 45 x 30cm. Cover with a few more sheets to make 4 layers, brushing with melted butter as above.

These beignets are one of those sticky, Middle Eastern-style desserts with lots of honey and nuts. Rather than the usual heavy pastries, however, they are light and fluffy little fritters.

cream cheese beignets with walnut honey

SERVES 4–6

450g cream cheese
25g caster sugar
Zest of ½ lemon
150g plain flour, sifted
2 eggs
Vegetable oil, for deep-frying
150ml clear honey
75g walnuts, chopped
Icing sugar, for dusting

Put the cheese, sugar and lemon zest in a bowl and beat together until smooth. Stir in the flour a little at a time, until thoroughly combined. Beat in the eggs one at a time, then set aside and leave to stand for up to 1 hour.

Put the vegetable oil in a deep-fat fryer or large saucepan and heat to 190°C, 375°F. Drop heaped teaspoonfuls of the cheese mixture into the hot oil a few at a time and fry for about 2 minutes, until golden and puffed up. Drain on kitchen paper and keep warm while you cook the rest. Heat the honey and walnuts in a pan until just warm. Dust the cheese beignets with icing sugar and serve with the walnut honey alongside.

Pecan pie is virtually America's national dessert. The addition of blue cheese makes an interesting variation. I like to serve the pie warm with lashings of double cream.

cashel blue & pecan pie

SERVES 4

½ quantity of sweet pastry (see p21)
Flour, for dusting
65g unsalted butter
4 tablespoons golden syrup
100g Cashel Blue or similar mild blue
  cheese, cut into small cubes
150g soft brown sugar
3 eggs
2 tablespoons rum
½ teaspoon vanilla extract
A pinch of salt
150g pecan nuts

Alternative cheese
If you prefer a stronger cheese, you could use Roquefort or Gorgonzola

Preheat the oven to 190°C, 375°F, gas 5. Roll out the pastry on a lightly floured surface until it is 3mm thick and use to line a 23cm flan tin, 2.5cm deep. Prick the base with a fork, line with greaseproof paper and fill with baking beans. Bake blind for 10 minutes, then remove the paper and beans and bake for a further 5 minutes. Remove from the oven and reduce the temperature to 180°C, 350°F, gas 4.

Heat the butter and golden syrup in a pan, add half the cheese and stir until melted. In a bowl, whisk together the sugar, eggs, rum, vanilla and salt. Add the pecan nuts and then stir into the syrup and cheese mixture. Add the remaining cheese and pour the mixture into the pastry case. Bake for about 30 minutes, until just set.

Made with Neufchâtel cheese, this delicate, sweet version of croque monsieur is not unlike pain perdu, or French toast. Although it can be served for dessert, it also makes a good brunch dish or summer breakfast. Neufchâtel is a creamy, fresh-tasting cheese from Normandy, best eaten young.

croque mademoiselle

SERVES 4

90g Neufchâtel
1 tablespoon Grand Marnier
Zest of 1/2 orange
3 tablespoons caster sugar
8 slices of brioche (see page 22),
  crusts removed
250g raspberries
2 eggs, beaten
150ml double cream
150ml milk
1 teaspoon ground cinnamon
50g unsalted butter
Icing sugar, for dusting

Alternative cheeses
If Neufchâtel is too strong for you,
replace it with quark or firm ricotta

Mix together the Neufchâtel, Grand Marnier, orange zest and 1 tablespoon of the sugar. Spread this mixture evenly over the slices of brioche. Top 4 slices with the raspberries, packing them tightly into the cheese, then sandwich together with the remaining brioche.

Beat together the eggs, cream, milk, cinnamon and remaining sugar and pour into a shallow dish. Dip the sandwiches into this mixture on both sides. Heat the butter in a large frying pan and cook the sandwiches for about 2 minutes on each side, until golden. Remove and drain on kitchen paper, then dust liberally with icing sugar. Serve the Croques Mademoiselles immediately, with some lightly whipped cream.

PG TIPS
You could substitute white bread for the brioche, although the flavour won't be quite as good. Some supermarkets stock light toast breads, which would work better than plain white bread.

This tart is a speciality of the Poitou region in France, where it is made with goat's cheese, as here, though you could substitute cream cheese.

tourte de poitou

SERVES 6

1/2 quantity of sweet pastry (see p 21)
Flour, for dusting
175g soft, unsalted goat's cheese,
  such as Sainte-Maure
3 eggs
100g caster sugar
2 tablespoons double cream
3 tablespoons finely chopped
  candied fruit
Zest of 1 orange
1 tablespoon pistachio nuts, skinned

Preheat the oven to 190°C, 375°F, gas 5. Roll out the pastry on a lightly floured surface until it is 3mm thick and use to line a 20cm flan tin. Prick the base with a fork, line with greaseproof paper and fill with baking beans. Bake blind for 10 minutes, then remove the paper and beans and return to the oven for 5 minutes longer.

Meanwhile chop the skinned pistachio nuts. Beat together all the remaining ingredients in a bowl until thoroughly combined. Pour into the pastry shell and return to the oven to bake for 45 minutes, until the top is a deep golden brown. Serve warm or, if you prefer, cold.

PG TIPS
To skin pistachio nuts, put them on a baking tray in a fairly hot oven for 1–2 minutes, then place them in a clean tea towel and rub gently to loosen the skins. Leave to cool, then peel off the skins.

Fillings for baked peaches are legion, but this combination of soft, fresh cheese, bitter chocolate and almond biscuits is especially good. Apricots can be prepared in the same way.

baked amaretti peaches with **ricotta** & bitter chocolate

SERVES 4

300ml dry white wine
4 tablespoons Amaretto liqueur
  (optional)
100g caster sugar
$\frac{1}{2}$ teaspoon vanilla extract or
  1 vanilla pod, split open
4 large, ripe peaches
4 tablespoons firm ricotta
50g amaretti biscuits,
  crushed into small pieces
2 tablespoons grated bitter chocolate
  (use plain chocolate with at least
  70% cocoa solids)
2 tablespoons semi-whipped
  double cream

Preheat the oven to 220°C, 425°F, gas 7. Bring the wine, Amaretto liqueur, if using, sugar and vanilla to the boil in a pan and boil for 5 minutes to form a light syrup. Add the peaches and poach for 1 minute. Remove the peaches with a slotted spoon and drain well, then slip off their skins. Cut the peaches in half, following the indentation that runs around their circumference. Twist each peach to loosen both halves and then remove the stone. Using a teaspoon, carefully scoop out a little of the flesh to enlarge the cavity.

In a bowl, mix together the ricotta, crushed amaretti and chocolate, then fold in the cream. Fill the peach halves with this mixture and place them in a baking dish that is just large enough to hold them in a single layer. Pour a little of the poaching syrup into the dish around the peaches and bake for 5–8 minutes, until golden. Serve immediately, with a good vanilla ice-cream.

PG TIPS
Freeze any leftover poaching syrup to make a delicately flavoured peach sorbet. An ideal way to enjoy this dessert all year round is to buy your peaches in the summer and bottle them in syrup for storing. They are also delicious served in their syrup with vanilla ice-cream.

This marriage of sweet and salty flavours is common in Mediterranean countries. I like to serve some crème fraîche with the turnovers, which makes for a nice contrast of temperatures.

cretan **sheep's milk** turnovers with melted honey

SERVES 4

125g Greek feta
40g cream cheese
1 egg, beaten
50g softened unsalted butter
1/4 teaspoon ground cinnamon
Juice of 1/4 lemon
2 tablespoons chopped fresh mint
Vegetable oil, for deep-frying
Icing sugar, for dusting
150ml honey, warmed
150ml crème fraîche (optional)

For the pastry
225g plain flour, plus extra
  for dusting
25g caster sugar
25g unsalted butter at room
  temperature, diced
About 150ml water

To make the pastry, sift the flour into a bowl, stir in the sugar, then rub in the butter pieces with your fingertips to give a coarse, sandy texture. Stir in enough water to make a soft, pliable dough. Turn out on to a lightly floured work surface and knead for 4–5 minutes, until smooth and elastic.

Place the feta in a bowl and crush it to a coarse pulp with a fork. Add the cream cheese and egg and beat together until smooth. Next, beat in the butter and cinnamon, then the lemon juice and chopped mint. Set aside in the refrigerator until required.

Roll the pastry out as thinly as possible on a lightly floured surface. Cut out 16–20 rounds with a 7.5cm pastry cutter. Put about 1 tablespoon of the feta filling on one half of each pastry round, brush the edges with water, then fold over and seal well to make turnovers. Place them in the refrigerator for 30 minutes to firm up.

Meanwhile, pour the vegetable oil into a deep-fat fryer or a deep saucepan and heat to 180–190°C, 350–375°F. Carefully slip the turnovers into the hot oil, a few at a time, and cook for about 2 minutes or until golden, turning them occasionally. Take out and drain on kitchen paper to remove excess oil. Keep warm while you fry the remaining turnovers. Place the turnovers on a serving dish, sift over a little icing sugar and drizzle with warm melted honey. Serve immediately, with crème fraîche if you like.

PG TIPS
Try to find a good Greek honey to use in this recipe. If time is of the essence, you could try using filo pastry instead. The result will be almost as good, although the turnovers will be a little crispy.

chapter 8 **alternative cheeseboard**

This sweet yet savoury preparation makes a great addition to a cheese board as well as a delicious alternative to a dessert. Dried cranberries and other varieties of dried fruits can easily replace the cherries.

baked **camembert** with dried cherries & caramel pecans

SERVES 4

100ml kirsch liquor
75g dried cherries
A whole small Camembert in
  its wooden box
100g caster sugar
100ml water
50g pecan nuts, coarsely broken
  into pieces

Heat the kirsch in a small pan with the cherries until it boils. Remove from the heat, transfer to a bowl and leave to cool overnight in the fridge. Remove the cherries and dry off any excess liquid.

Take the camembert from its box, remove the paper wrapping and, using a small knife, insert a dozen or so tiny slits into the cheese liberally over the surface. Press the cherries into the slits.

Preheat the oven to 200ºC, 400ºF, gas 6. Arrange the camembert on a wire rack over a foil-lined baking sheet.

Place the sugar and water in a heavy based pan then warm over a low heat to dissolve the sugar. Increase the heat and let it boil until the sugar takes on a light golden caramel colour. Add the pecan pieces and spoon the nut caramel over the camembert.

Place the cheese in the oven for 10–12 minutes, until the cheese is heated through and begins to soften. Cool to room temperature before serving. Cut into wedges.

A quick and simple method of marinating cheese, with basil, olive oil and garlic. I like to serve it as part of a cheeseboard but it also makes a good light starter accompanied by a small crisp salad and some bread.

simple marinated **chèvre** in basil oil

SERVES 4

4 crottin de Chavignol or aged
  Chabis goat's cheeses, cut
  horizontally in half
1 bay leaf
6 black peppercorns, lightly crushed
2 garlic cloves, crushed
1 handful of fresh basil leaves
125ml extra-virgin olive oil, warmed
Salt

Alternative cheeses
A creamy Camembert or Brie,
cut into slices 1cm thick,
or Roubiliac goat's cheese balls

Place the cheese halves in a dish just large enough to hold them in one layer and put the bay leaf and peppercorns on top. Blitz the garlic, basil and olive oil together in a blender to form a fairly liquid sauce and then season with salt. Pour the basil oil over the cheese, cover and leave in a cool place for about 6 hours. It will keep for about a week in the refrigerator, but bring to room temperature before serving.

Serve this delicious cheese preserve with a good walnut bread.

pressed cheese with dried fruits

SERVES 4

4 crottin de Chavignol or aged
  Chabis goat's cheeses, cut
  horizontally in half
50g dried figs, cut into quarters
50g prunes, cut in half
3 sprigs of fresh thyme
3 bay leaves
6 black peppercorns
6 tablespoons prune eau de vie
  or cognac
Olive oil

Place 2 of the cheese halves in a sterilized 500ml preserving jar and scatter over a third each of the figs and prunes, plus a sprig of thyme, a bay leaf and 2 peppercorns. Sprinkle over 1$\frac{1}{2}$ tablespoons of the eau de vie or cognac. Put 2 more cheese halves on top and repeat these layers until all the ingredients are used up, ending with a layer of cheese and pressing it down well. The cheese should be tightly packed. Sprinkle over the remaining eau de vie or cognac. Pour in enough olive oil to cover the cheese and then leave in a cool place, but not the refrigerator, for at least a week. Store in the refrigerator once opened.

This cheese dip from Hungary is usually made from a soft sheep's milk cheese, which is not always easy to obtain, so I have substituted cream cheese. Crisp biscuits are great with this, although a selection of vegetable crudités is also very good. Liptauer keeps for about a week in the refrigerator.

liptauer

SERVES 4

225g cream cheese, such as
  Philadelphia or fresh Explorateur
4 tablespoons soured cream
50g softened unsalted butter
2 teaspoons superfine capers,
  drained
2 canned anchovy fillets, finely
  chopped

1 tablespoon chopped fresh chives
1 tablespoon mild paprika, plus
extra for dusting
1 teaspoon caraway seeds
1/2 teaspoon mild mustard
Salt

Blend all the ingredients together briefly in a food processor or beat them together in a bowl. Cover and leave overnight in the refrigerator to allow the flavours to infuse. To serve, adjust the seasoning if necessary, transfer to a serving dish and dust the top with a little paprika.

I love this Lebanese dish, which has been traditionally prepared in the mountain villages for centuries. It is both simple to make and a wonderful appetiser, served with garlic bread or grilled pitta breads.

shanklish

SERVES 4

350g fresh goat's cheese
1 garlic clove, crushed
1 red chilli, deseeded and
  finely diced
2 tablespoons roughly chopped fresh
  flat-leaf parsley
1 medium red onion, finely diced
3 ripe but firm tomatoes, diced
3 tablespoons extra virgin olive oil
Freshly cracked black pepper

Place the goat's cheese in a bowl and lightly crush with a fork along with the garlic and chilli. Stir in the parsley, onion and tomato and carefully mix together, taking care not to break up the tomato pieces. Season well with black pepper and transfer to a serving dish. Drizzle over the olive oil and serve.

PG TIPS
In Lebanon and Syria, Shanklish is often mashed with cooked hard boiled egg or with cucumber and mint. Both are equally delicious.

Serve this chutney with a selection of cheeses and some crusty bread. If you are using the sweeter red gooseberries, you will need the smaller amount of sugar listed in the ingredients. Although you can store it in preserving jars for months, a good chutney will also keep for one month unsealed in the refrigerator and will, in fact, improve in flavour.

gooseberry & green peppercorn **chutney**

MAKES ABOUT 900G

600g fresh green or red
  gooseberries
2 onions, chopped
1 garlic clove, crushed
1/2 teaspoon mustard powder
1 teaspoon lemon juice
300ml cider vinegar or
  white wine vinegar
175g raisins
75–275g soft brown sugar
A large pinch of salt
2 tablespoons green peppercorns

Put the gooseberries, onions, garlic, mustard and lemon juice in a preserving pan and pour over two-thirds of the vinegar. Bring to the boil, then reduce the heat and simmer for about 45 minutes, stirring occasionally, until thick. Add the raisins, salt, sugar and the rest of the vinegar. Stir over a low heat until the sugar has dissolved, then simmer for up to 1 hour, stirring frequently, until thick and syrupy. Stir in the peppercorns, then remove from the heat. Either leave to cool, then store in the refrigerator for up to a month, or pour immediately into hot sterilized jars, seal and store in a cool, dark place.

The pears are cooked quite briefly so that they keep their shape, resulting in a nice chunky chutney. It is very good served with a mature farmhouse Cheddar such as Montgomery's or Keen's.

saffron pear **chutney**

MAKES ABOUT 900G

2 cooking apples, peeled & grated
125g onions, finely chopped
125g sultanas
Juice & zest of 4 oranges
300g granulated sugar
1 teaspoon ground cinnamon
1 teaspoon freshly grated nutmeg
1 teaspoon cayenne pepper
2 pinches of saffron strands

1 1/2 teaspoons salt
50g fresh ginger root, grated
300ml white wine vinegar
750g pears, peeled, cored &
  roughly chopped
350g tomatoes, skinned, deseeded
  & diced

Put all the ingredients except the pears and tomatoes in a preserving pan and simmer for about 30 minutes, stirring from time to time, until the mixture is reduced to a syrup. It should be thick enough to coat the back of a spoon. Add the pears and tomatoes and cook for 10–15 minutes, until the pears are just soft. Pour into hot sterilized jars and seal, then store in a cool, dark place.

cheeseboard (clockwise from top): capricorn, sainte-maure, keen's cheddar, golden cross, boulettes d'avesnes, roquefort societé, reblochon

A delicately flavoured pickle that makes an interesting accompaniment to cheese. Although this recipe uses white grapes, you could substitute red ones. Remember that good-quality vinegar is essential for making a good pickle.

sweet & sour grape **pickle**

MAKES ABOUT 1 LITRE

750g seedless white grapes
10 sprigs of fresh tarragon
500ml champagne vinegar or
 white wine vinegar
175ml honey
1 teaspoon salt

Wash the grapes well and then dry them. Put them in a large sterilized preserving jar with the sprigs of tarragon. Boil the vinegar and honey together for 2 minutes, then add the salt and pour the mixture over the grapes. Seal the jar immediately. For best results, store in a cool dark place for up to 1 month before opening.

This delicately flavoured loaf is one of my favourites and a real winner at the Lanesborough, where we serve it as an accompaniment to our cheese selection. I like it slightly warm with my cheese.

lanesborough dried fig & fennel seed **bread**

MAKES 1 LOAF

15g fresh yeast or 1/2 sachet
 Easyblend yeast
125ml water
250g strong brown flour
1/2 teaspoon salt
15g unsalted butter
150g dried figs, cut into strips
 about 5mm wide
1 1/2 teaspoons fennel seeds

If using fresh yeast, put it in a small bowl, pour on the water and mix until smooth. Sift the flour and salt into another bowl and rub in the butter, then make a well in the centre and add the yeast and water mixture. Stir in the flour to form a soft dough. If using Easyblend yeast, stir it into the flour after rubbing in the butter and then pour in the water.

Turn the dough out on to a lightly floured surface and knead for 8–10 minutes, until smooth and elastic. Add the dried figs and fennel seeds and knead for 1 minute longer, until incorporated. Do not overknead the dough at this stage or the figs will disintegrate. Leave to relax for about 5 minutes, then shape into an oval loaf, place on a greased baking sheet and cover with a clean damp tea towel. Leave in a warm place for about 50 minutes, until it has doubled in size.

Preheat the oven to 220°C, 425°F, gas 7. Bake the loaf for 30 minutes, or until it is golden brown on top and sounds hollow when tapped underneath. Cool on a wire rack.

breads (clockwise from top): stilton bread, mozzarella & sun-dried tomato bread, lanesborough dried fig & fennel seed bread, cheddar & onion loaf, cheddar & onion loaf, stilton bread (centre)

index